MW01712521

At Her Feet: the playscript

Nadia Davids

with additional material by Keren Hoy

OXFORD
UNIVERSITY PRESS
SOUTHERN AFRICA

OXFORD
UNIVERSITY PRESS

SOUTHERN AFRICA

Oxford University Press Southern Africa (Pty) Ltd

Vasco Boulevard, Goodwood, Cape Town, Republic of South Africa
P O Box 12119, N1 City, 7463, Cape Town, Republic of South Africa

Oxford University Press Southern Africa (Pty) Ltd is a subsidiary of Oxford University Press, Great Clarendon Street, Oxford OX2 6DP.

The Press, a department of the University of Oxford, furthers the University's objective of excellence in research, scholarship, and education by publishing worldwide in

Oxford New York

Auckland Cape Town Dar es Salaam Hong Kong Karachi
Kuala Lumpur Madrid Melbourne Mexico City Nairobi
New Delhi Shanghai Taipei Toronto

With offices in

Argentina Austria Brazil Chile Czech Republic France Greece
Guatemala Hungary Italy Japan Poland Portugal Singapore South Korea
Switzerland Turkey Ukraine Vietnam

Oxford is a registered trade mark of Oxford University Press in the UK and in certain other countries

Published in South Africa
by Oxford University Press Southern Africa (Pty) Ltd, Cape Town

At Her Feet: the playscript
ISBN 978 0 19 599254 0

First published by Zebra Press/Oshun Books in 2006
First published by Oxford University Press Southern Africa (Pty) Ltd 2009
Second impression 2013

Enquiries regarding professional or amateur stage performances should be addressed to Nadia Davids at nadiadavids77@gmail.com

Publishing Manager: Megan Hall
Assistant Commissioning Editor: Helga Schaberg
Editor: Arlene Stephenson
Cover and book designer: Samantha Rowles
Cover photographs: Ruphin Coudyzer
Photographs: Ruphin Coudyzer, Andrew Michau (Tahira Hussien, page 19)

Set in Minion Pro Regular 11 pt on 12,5 pt by Baseline Publishing Services
Printed and bound by ABC Press, Cape Town
119316

Acknowledgements
The authors and publisher gratefully acknowledge permission to reproduce copyright material in this book. Every effort has been made to trace copyright holders, but if any copyright infringements have been made, the publisher would be grateful for information that would enable any omissions or errors to be corrected in subsequent impressions. Photographs by Ruphin Coudyzer FPPSA – www.ruphin.com

Contents

Acknowledgements

My thanks and love to my sister Leila, who held all the words first.

I am grateful to Quanita and Andrew – fellow travellers and sandwich eaters – who believed in and committed to the work from the start.

The work was able to play and travel through the institutional support of the South African National Arts Council and the Prince Claus Fund of Holland, and because of the infrastructural support of the University of Cape Town.

I am entirely indebted to the response of communities in Cape Town; it is because of them that these monologues became a conversation.

Foreword by Gabeba Baderoon

"Looking at me like you look at them"

At Her Feet is a one-woman play consisting of interlocking monologues by six Muslim women. This is a play that is a pleasure to read, to listen to, to see, to feel come alive. It talks about difficult things – as women do with one another. Watching and reading, we form the hidden other that is the audience; we sit in the interior spaces of the play while important things happen close to us.

At Her Feet displays a startlingly true ear for dialogue and tone of voice. It feels as if the writer has been present in our homes, our conversations, our inner reflections. At the same time, the language of the play tells of other rhythms, other places, other languages – Afrikaans, Arabic, American English, the language of youth, of politics, of possessions. Its scenes are offered in textured and deliberately fractured ways, using allusions, memories, and poetry. At the same time, it avoids earnestness. It is funny, clever, and energetic.

The play juxtaposes different women who have the same name attached to them – that of Islam. It puts them next to one another, inside one another's assumptions[1] and prejudices. It leaves no comfortable assumptions untouched. It inscribes on one actress's body different accents, beliefs, doubts, confessions, silences. As readers, we revisit our own beliefs, the basis of our recognition, our laughter.

Nadia Davids writes from experience, yet with a reflective quality that avoids any simple notion of identity as sameness. In its multiple forms – poetry, music, dance, and the lyrical words of its six characters – the play displays the talents of a writer whose creativity takes whatever shape is most apt. The author uses the elasticity of theatre – its immediacy and intimacy with the audience, its collaborative[2] nature – to take her characters into the world. To me, a Muslim feminist encountering the complex personal and ethical choices with which the characters engage, the play offers a space of empathy[3] and solace.[4]

1 **assumptions:** things that are accepted without proof
2 **collaborative:** involving several people or groups of people working together
3 **empathy:** ability to understand and share in someone else's feelings
4 **solace:** comfort

This is a play that is embedded in the details of Muslim women's lives. The characters are related to one another as mother and daughter, aunt and niece, cousins and friends. The rhythms of fasting, praying, Eid celebrations, cooking, work, and politics mark their speech. Their relationships with one another, the intertwining of religion and ordinary life, the different calendars of the body, the mosque, the kitchen, funerals, childhood, marriage, friendship, politics, sin, transgression, shame, fear, war, solitude, history – these form the material of the characters' lives and of the play.

In *At Her Feet*, Nadia Davids explores the relations between race, politics and religion, and the intertwining local and global tendrils of a South African Muslim identity. The play's energy, its power, lie in the use of familiar themes associated with Islam – patriarchal men[5] and veiled, suffering woman – taken in unexpected directions.

The vision of Islam conveyed in *At Her Feet* accommodates both the horror Sara feels at seeing an "honour" killing on television, and an experience of Islam as part of resistance to power. Ayesha, the politically engaged character who shares the name of the wife of the Prophet, a warrior and leader in the earliest Islamic community, describes Islam in terms that combine spirituality, politics, subversion, poetry, and music. In the play, we also see Sara's connectedness with Muslim women in other parts of the world, Tahira's consumerism at Eid, and Auntie Kariema's derogatory comments about Indian Muslims. Through the metaphor of a *tawaaf*[6] around a shopping mall, the author perfectly juxtaposes the circumambulation[7] of the Ka'aba[8] with the rival resonance of consumerism for Muslim boys. Indeed, one of the points the play illustrates is that its Muslim characters are not exempt from internal contradiction, or even complicity with racism.

The play is framed by poetry, from the poetic Hadith,[9] which gives it its title, and the excerpt from "Cape Town, Jerusalem" by Rustum Kozain, to three other poems, "The Scarf", "Eid Day" and "Ms Islam". Poetry draws attention to language that is not direct and factual, but lyrical, resonant and layered. Such language unsettles a single

---

5 **patriarchal men:** men who give power and control only to men
6 ***tawaaf*:** parade; refers specifically to a route around the Ka'aba during the haj
7 **circumambulation:** movement around a holy or sacred object
8 **Ka'aba:** square building in Mecca, Saudi Arabia; Muslims pray facing it, and it is the focal point of the haj, or pilgrimage
9 **Hadith:** sayings of the Prophet Mohamed

meaning, whether we are engaging with representations of Islam, or imperatives[10] within Islam. *At Her Feet* traverses the spaces between these concepts, and between the lyrical monologues by Azra and her mother that open and close the play.

At Her Feet contains lines that will always stay with me.

It opens with the monologue of Azra al Jamal, a young Jordanian woman who has been stoned to death by the male members of her community, speaking after she has been killed. With the declaration that opens the play, "My name is Azra al Jamal, and I have just been killed", we are invited into all the possible and impossible worlds of Muslim women. The play allows us to enter the silence of the character.

The theme of the veil – familiar, vexed,[11] illusory,[12] tempting – is rendered in the subtle views of the play's characters. Here, too, the play signals the complexity of the issues it addresses. In her politically engaged vision of Islam, Ayesha flourishes the incantatory[13] list of religious and historical figures that she claims as her heritage, yet also draws an intellectual veil over her uncertainties.

Knowing the intense scrutiny experienced by Muslim women who choose to wear a veil, the play declines to reveal the secrets of an "authentic" insider. Instead, the beauty and pleasure of scarves is explored alongside the acknowledgement that, as a Muslim woman, Sara is affected by the way she is seen when she wears a scarf. She articulates this dilemma powerfully: "Maybe I don't want you looking at me, like you look at them."

The most hard-earned, most memorable line in the play is delivered by Auntie Kariema, whom we meet as the garrulous,[14] funny, prejudiced foil[15] of the serious and central figure of Sara. Smoking a secret cigarette, Auntie Kariema recalls that when she lost her mother when she was ten, she was prevented from joining her father and walking to the cemetery to bury her mother because of her gender. The unforgotten and unassuaged[16] pain of not being present at her mother's burial – "I needed to bury my mother" – leads Auntie Kariema to realise that there is a direct connection between her desires and those of the dead Jordanian girl. So it is Auntie Kariema

10 **imperatives:** commandments
11 **vexed:** annoying; worrying
12 **illusory:** based on something imaginary
13 **incantatory:** words spoken or sung for their magical effect
14 **garrulous:** very talkative
15 **foil:** person who, by contrast, makes others seem better
16 **unassuaged:** not soothed or lessened

who travels the longest distance in the play, to say, with profound empathy for Azra, "I wanted to walk and she wanted to talk."

I have sat in the audience watching this play and feeling a vast wholeness grip the audience as the lines have unfolded, presenting surprising characters we end up loving and wanting more of, and those whose interior reflections sound exactly like our own. Simultaneously, I have felt so recognised, so directly addressed, that I might have been completely alone. The play's compelling intelligence has led to rapturous responses from both audiences and critics. Perhaps in this rapture there was relief – relief that at last we had received a work that was equal to the fluidity and difficulty and laughter of our lives.

Gabeba Baderoon
Sweden, November 2005

Playwright's notes

This is a play about women.

It is a collection of stories about mothers, daughters, aunts, cousins, friends and sisters, all struggling to reach each other across different divides.

When I first began to think about writing a play about Muslim women, the world was reeling[17] from the events of September 11, 2001, and their aftermath. Afghan women were constantly on televisual display, and Amina Lawal's[18] tragic circumstances were being played out in the midst of a media fracas.[19]

My sister Leila was deeply engrossed in a Masters thesis that examined Muslim women's identity in Cape Town. I was one of her interview subjects, and she began, in her gentle and exploratory way, to pose questions to me about my race, place, citizenship and experience, all the while encouraging me to narrate my story. One day, a friend of mine began speaking to me about an honour killing in Jordan; as we talked, we ran a gamut[20] of emotions: outrage, disbelief, anger, and, eventually, hopeless helplessness.

I began to imagine the victim of the killing, her death, her life, her choices, and began to think about how different Muslim women in Cape Town might respond to her murder. Growing up Muslim in Cape Town, one feels a strange diasporic[21] link to the Middle East, a belief in a collective Ummah;[22] but, at the same time, there is an awareness that our traditions and practices differ widely. Islam, and especially women in Islam post-9/11, seemed to be the subject of a global and heated conversation, and I wanted, in the interests of diversity, to offer a different story. Today, seven years later, the world has shifted, contracted, regressed, progressed; there is certainly a more informed debate about what constitutes the scarf, the veil, the place Muslim women occupy in our global imaginations; we have

17 **reeling:** feeling shocked and upset
18 **Amina Lawal:** Nigerian woman who, in an Islamic shari'ah court in 2002, was sentenced to death by stoning for adultery and conceiving a child. The ruling was overturned in 2004.
19 **fracas:** quarrel; argument; row
20 **ran a gamut:** experienced the complete range
21 **diasporic:** literally "dispersed", in this case referring to Muslims who feel, in a sense, removed from their true spiritual "home"
22 **Ummah:** community of Muslims bound together by ties of religion

entered a more hopeful era in geo-politics, and yet .... Earlier this year when Gaza was bombed, I was shocked. Not necessarily by the bombings, but by persistent language of "collateral damage" used for dead women and children. This is a term that has gained immense popularity since the second invasion of the Persian Gulf; it is a phrase that insinuates[23] at best collective political guilt, at worst, a casual insistence that those lives just aren't worth very much. Another story, just as horrifying: in April of this year, a Pakistani girl of seventeen was flogged in a public square for talking to a married man. Two men held her and a third beat her until she screamed, "Rather just kill me – I cannot bear the pain." One of the men was her brother. These are difficult stories; hard to confront and to try and contemplate. But in today's globalised world of interconnected interdependence and easily available information, we cannot afford to switch off or cop out.[24]

The moment I decided to begin writing this piece, I bought a hardcover A4 book and covered it in a silk scarf, which held the words inside it in a patterned embrace. The book was a journal of my intentions. Coupled with the monologues are lists or manifestos[25] that state a need to demystify[26] Muslim women, to offer multiple ways of seeing them, and to attend to the problems and dynamics that exist within various Cape Town communities.

I felt that a one-woman show, in which six different characters with different modes of expression (movement, hip-hop, poetry, monologue) inscribed on a single body, might be an interesting way of shifting audiences from seeing Muslim women as veiled, mysterious, and homogeneous[27] entities. I began to speak to Quanita Adams about the possibility of her performing the work, and was delighted at the interface between our perspectives, and the genuine understanding she had of the work and its many meanings.

But the political impulse was in many ways just that first feeling, the initial impetus, because the work is about women: the big, difficult questions they face, their small but important triumphs, and the journeys that they make towards each other.

While this play is not autobiographical in the traditional sense,

23 **insinuates:** hints at or suggests something unpleasant
24 **cop out:** avoid or stop doing something we should be doing; not take responsibility
25 **manifestos:** public statements of policies and principles
26 **demystify:** make clear and easy to understand by using simple language to explain
27 **homogeneous:** all the same; identical

it draws on composites[28] of people I have known all my life, and plays homage to a place I call home. The issues that I wanted to trace around culture, tradition, religion, prejudice, inalienable[29] rights, gender bias, and discrimination are not in any way endemic[30] to Muslim communities. I believe I would have written about these things through different stories had I been born into a different set of circumstances – I have simply used the prism I have been given.

While the play and its details are located in a specific place, I think the stories these characters offer – the way they laugh and cry through them, and the emotional legacies they leave – are more about finding commonalities and shared histories with their audiences than creating difference.

Nadia Davids
New York, 2009

---

28 **composites:** in this case, characterisation made up of a number of different parts or aspects
29 **inalienable:** not able to be given away or taken away
30 **endemic:** found only in a certain group, in this instance, Muslims

Interview with Nadia Davids by Leila Davids

Leila Davids is a social development researcher who holds a Masters degree in Research Psychology from the University of Cape Town. Her dissertation on the identities of Muslim women in Cape Town formed the academic platform for the development of At Her Feet. *Leila and Nadia are not only sisters, but close friends and co-creators, who have collaborated on various projects since childhood. This interview first appeared in the* Annual Review of Islam in South Africa (ARISA).

At Her Feet is a play about the diverse experiences of Muslim women, both locally and globally. Women are often made invisible or silent – other voices speak to them, at them, and for them. This play breaks this silence, presenting the words and feelings of a group of characters, most of whom are from Cape Town, in a way that is non-judgemental and sincere. It uses a variety of art forms to do so – poetry, music, movement, and speech suggest the wide range of experiences and opinions of these women. The play creates and explores links that "go beyond language", that arise from the sometimes surprising connections between its characters.

At the conclusion of the interview that follows, Nadia asks "Why are Muslim women not given the space to air their doubts and beliefs?" This is the question that drives the play, and she answers it by focusing on what women have to say. Her play opens with the stoning to death of a Jordanian girl, Azra al Jamal, whose story forms the thread that makes these connections, with each character interacting with Azra in different ways. Woven through the stories that the women tell us are burning issues of culture, belonging and exclusion, revealed through the sharing of happiness, sadness, and respect.

At Her Feet has made a fresh space for theatrical expressions of Muslim culture, and Muslim women's experiences in particular, that does not shy away from painful issues such as gender violence and racism, or retreat from joyful articulation and humour.

The following interview takes the form of a dialogue between Nadia, my sister, and myself, two Muslim-born women from Cape Town. We did the interview in 2002 after the first commercial run of

At Her Feet at the Baxter Theatre in Cape Town, and it was published in a slightly different format in the journal *Annual Review of Islam in South Africa* (December 2002), for the Centre for Contemporary Islam at the University of Cape Town.

Leila: Tell me what made you write this piece, and what processes you went through while writing it.

Nadia: The process of writing this play was very much about an internal impulse. I am at a point in my life where I am trying in a very conscious way to address the issue of how it is that I relate to the outside world based on certain identities that have been prescribed. For me, this used to be very much a race issue, based on the fact that I am a South African woman who is not white and not black, but classified as coloured. After September 11, this became very much about where I positioned myself as a Muslim woman, or as someone who happened to be born into the Muslim faith. This was highlighted for me by your research on issues around what it is to be a South African Muslim woman, and how this can be a political subjectivity for some women and a spiritual link for others.

So my work is a practical exploration of certain ideological[31] and theoretical ideas that you have been developing. I was also responding to talks with Muslim women, my family and friends, which sent me into a deeper space of reflection on these issues. I wanted to focus on certain taboo issues, including issues that were specific to a Cape Town Muslim context. We have such an incredibly fractured, creolised society,[32] subject to so many different pulls and influences all the time. Just like any other society, actually. It feels so specific because it is under-explored.

My friend told me about this honour killing in Jordan that she had seen on television, and it was just so frightening. I began to wonder what happens when a Muslim woman living in Cape Town, in what is essentially a highly diasporic space (because we have this extraordinarily strong psychological link with the Middle East), who has access to all kinds of education and forms

31 **ideological:** based on a set of beliefs
32 **creolised society:** society that has been influenced and changed by another society

of communication, and has a fairly questioning mind – what happens when you see something like that done in the name of your faith? And what happens when you see a girl or a woman, and by virtue of the fact that they are scarfed, you make a very strong imagistic connection with them? That is when I started to write about Azra, because I needed to go through a process of establishing a relationship with those women.

Leila: How did Azra become the thread that led to all the other women in the play?

Nadia: It's very clear that the play is an imagined space. It is book-ended by two symbolic, lyrical, surreal[33] slices that present my perceptions of Middle Eastern women, probably a very flawed perception. The point of the play is how we imagine them here, in Cape Town. I think it's quite clear that if one of the women in the play who is not Middle Eastern was stoned to death, the reaction would be very different. I want people in Cape Town to realise that there should not be double standards of freedom for here and the women over there, merely because they appear to be leading a more Islamic life.

Leila: Your perceptions about Muslim women have been pivotal to the creative process of this production. How have those perceptions shifted?

Nadia: I remember a group of about eight very conservatively dressed women in their forties and fifties came to watch the play. I must admit that something inside me tightened up when I saw them before the show. I hoped none of them would be offended or upset, because it is not my aim to be disrespectful. I felt so shamed by my own pre-judgement, because after the show, these women came up to me and hugged me. They thanked me for saying things that they themselves had not been able to say. That made the whole process worthwhile.

Leila: Do you think that there has been a generational shift? Is the fact that you can say these things because we have matured into adulthood in a culture that openly values freedom and justice?

33 **surreal:** more like a dream than reality

Nadia: I think it's not necessarily a generational shift in terms of Muslim society, I think it's a global generational shift, in which attempts have been made to accord women's freedoms the same space and importance as race freedom. For so long the dialogue on gender freedom has been subsumed by a racial one.[34] I think you see something similar in traditional African communities, where the same paradigm[35] is now being played out.

Leila: How did you address those issues in the play?

Nadia: Well, for one, through issues of veiling and hair and showing how in Cape Town with our notions about "genuine" hair and people who look more Muslim that others, I showed how we conflate[36] race issues with gender ones. The characters in the play have specific ways of dealing with these ideas, but I have tried to keep them nuanced and multi-dimensional. They are each composites of people I know. So Auntie Kariema is horrified that her university-educated niece, Sara, calls herself black and African when she has such long, straight hair. Sara in turn is grappling with her faith, trying to reconcile her cultural dictates with her very personal connection to God. Her friend Ayesha, who takes Islam very seriously, is Auntie Kariema's son's ex-girlfriend. Their break-up is preceded by his refusal to introduce Ayesha to Auntie Kariema because her hair is not straight. So Ayesha, in a theatrical display of defiance, purchases a long blonde wig and has tea with a stunned Auntie Kariema. The scene is hilarious, but at the same time very painful, and that pain is accessed because we know that hair is bound up in issues of shame that are pertinent to both gender and race identities.

Leila: Did you write the play with a specific audience in mind, one that would relate to those types of connection?

Nadia: Strangely, no. I wrote from my own experiences, and the stories told to me throughout my life, from when I was very little and confused because I attended a Christian school for most of the day and the Madressa[37] in the afternoons,

34 **subsumed by a racial one:** not considered separately but rather as part of racial issues
35 **paradigm:** pattern or model of how things should be done
36 **conflate:** put two or more things together to form something new
37 **Madressa:** Islamic school, Muslim school, or after-school Islamic instruction

through to the present and my interactions with people generally.

The play does have a very local feel. Certain characters speak words that perhaps people who are not Muslim or do not have that much contact with Muslims won't understand, but that is part of telling stories with honesty. You can't dictate language parameters and cater to an audience.

The film *Monsoon Wedding* is mentioned in the play, and I suppose, on reflection, it serves a dual purpose. It highlights the prejudice and discord that some people encounter between and within Muslim communities in Cape Town, the supposed Indian-Malay divide. It also illustrates the way art can transcend cultural boundaries, showing that you don't have to be an insider to relate to people and their joys and struggles; you don't have to be a woman to understand that being restricted from certain arenas is unfair. Emotions are sometimes effective tools of communication – a look can convey meaning without a word being spoken. Azra's mother says "there are no words for you now" and proclaims that her daughter is in Paradise and at the feet of the Infinitely Compassionate.

Leila: The title of the play is an obvious nod to a particular Hadith …

Nadia: I drew on religion to title the play because that is one of our strongest links to one another. These women are related through their religious heritage, however different, and regardless of whether they do or do not subscribe to it. Personally, that Hadith has played out in many ways for me; it has been a soundtrack in my mind whenever I see atrocities[38] against women being committed in the name of Islam.

Leila: Every character expresses strong, unwavering criticism of aspects of her own culture. How much do you think that reflects the way you understand women's resistance?

Nadia: Well, we all talk. In that talk and those conversations are moments of hesitation and moments of comprehension. Cultures and traditions are constantly changing, and women

38 **atrocities:** extremely wicked or cruel acts

debate among themselves and in public, but we also work things out introspectively. It is not endemic to Islam, or Muslim women in Cape Town. For every person in the world, whatever cultures they are straddling, there are things that work for them and things that do not. Why are Muslim women not given the space to air their doubts and beliefs?

Cape Town
2002

The play

The history of the play

At Her Feet was first performed at the Arena Theatre, at the Hiddingh campus of the University of Cape Town, in September 2002.

Written and directed by Nadia Davids
Performed by Quanita Adams
Lighting design by Andrew Michau

At Her Feet was subsequently performed in 2003 at the Warehouse Theatre for the Cape Town Festival, the Sanlam Studio at the Baxter Theatre, the Box Theatre at the Grahamstown Festival, the Market Theatre for the Women's Day Festival, the St Anne's Theatre Festival in Pietermaritzburg, and Pacoff's Huguenot Theatre in Bloemfontein.

In 2004, it was performed again at the Sanlam Studio at the Baxter Theatre, and also at the Maitisong Festival in Botswana, the State Theatre in Pretoria, the Frascati Theatre in Amsterdam, the Ars-Nova Theatre in New York, and at the Center for Political and Social Change through the Arts at New York University. In 2009 it was staged at the Market Theatre in Johannesburg.

Awards

Fleur du Cap Award for Best New Director, 2003: Nadia Davids; Fleur du Cap Award for Best Actress, 2003: Quanita Adams; awarded second place in the Cape Times Top Ten plays of 2002. *At Her Feet* received an honourable mention in the 2007 Noma Awards for outstanding literature published in South Africa.

Characters in order of appearance

Azra al Jamal	A young Jordanian Muslim woman, stoned to death in an "honour" killing
Sara Jacobs	The play's storyteller. She is a South African Muslim woman in her twenties who lives in Cape Town
Auntie Kariema	Sara's aunt, a middle-aged Muslim woman who lives in Cape Town and identifies herself as "Malay"
Ayesha	Sara's friend, a young Muslim feminist slam-poetess who lives in Cape Town
Tahira Hussein	Sara's cousin, a newly-married Indian-Muslim woman who works for a travel agency in Cape Town
Azra's mother	The Jordanian girl's mother

Quanita Adams as (clockwise from top left) *Azra, Auntie Kariema, Ayesha, and Tahira Hussein.*

… as I turn
from the stone's articulate act
and seek the sentence long enough
to house my tribe, even as I know
of neither's existence.

from "Cape Town, Jerusalem"
by Rustum Kozain

Paradise lies at the feet of mothers.
Hadith

At Her Feet: the playscript

Stage in darkness. Stage right is a plain wooden table and chair, stage left is a wooden stool, and a box with scarves in it. There are two metal hooks hanging from the rafters, stage left. The strains of tabla music[1] *can be heard. A blue light comes up, and we see a figure garbed in full hijab.*[2] *She begins to dance. The dance is a metaphorical enactment of a stoning, drawing on various Middle-Eastern movement motifs.*[3] *Eventually, the figure moves centre stage, in a spotlight, and falls gradually to her knees. The light changes, the blue light fades, and she takes off the burkha.*[4]

Azra al Jamal

My name is Azra. It means un-pierced pearl. It means that I am untouched. My name is for something pure and unsoiled. My name is Azra al Jamal, and I have just been killed. I have sat in the middle of a circle of forty men, and I have just been killed. I have felt my body break in different places, and pieces of bone scrape through skin, because there have been eighty hands throwing countless rocks at me for some time now. I have felt my mouth bleed softly against sand, dry enough to make me choke, too thin for me to clutch.

My name is Azra al Jamal and I have just been killed.

Because I spoke to a man who was not my father/brother/uncle/cousin, and now my father/brother/uncle/cousin has taken rocks and flung them, knocked me unconscious, smashed my teeth, made me beg and scream and say "I didn't mean to", but I did mean to, and my intention doesn't matter now, because I have no honour. And I have no voice. And it is as though my name, my name, Azra al Jamal, means nothing, because I have been ground into the sand. Curled up in an awkward zero, I am circling my own end. It's hot, and though

---

1 ***tabla music***: a type of Indian music that uses a pair of small hand drums fixed together
2 ***hijab***: (Arabic) veil or headscarf worn by traditionalist or orthodox Muslim women when in public
3 ***motifs***: repeated themes, or elements of design or movement
4 ***burkha***: long, loose garment that entirely covers the head, face, and body, and is worn by some orthodox Muslim women when in public

it is midday, all I can see is night. Bent over, halfway between prayer and nausea, I have been tracing the patterns of the desert sky for hours now. I have watched the stars, seen their geometry, heard them moan anxiously down at me, and felt my insides implode with every hardened blow. I have forgotten my name, so I ask you to remember it.

And somewhere – between voices shouting angrily and hands saving me from a worse fate in the afterlife – I know that it is still light. I remember that it is a clear day – that the sun is hanging persistently at the back of my neck, that light is pouring in over secrets. That there are no shadows, or doorways to hide in, that sharing words, using breath to make sounds, letting a voice come through the folds of this cloth, is not allowed. It is a clear day, lost somewhere in a dark time. It is a clear day. Anyone who walks by now can see what is happening to me.

Do you remember my name?

Azra *removes the hijab, and hangs the burkha on one of the hooks. Underneath she is wearing black pants and a top, and is now in the mode of* **Sara**[5]*, the storyteller. She is thoughtful and reflective, given to bursts of energetic impersonation when she describes a place or person.*

Sara Jacobs

She searches through the wooden box, delighting in the different fabrics, searching for the right scarf to recite her poem with.

THE SCARF
It begins with geometry –

A square folded half
three-tiered, naked edges,
a shape now formed
neither here nor there,
the legacy of Egypt
a dream for Pythagoras.

It begins with hair –

5 **Sara:** this is the most common spelling in the Arab world, where the first syllable is pronounced with a long *ah* vowel sound and not an *ê* as in English

Sara (Quanita Adams) searches for a scarf suitable to wear when reciting her poem.

The tissue of seduction
streaming dead tendrils
that writhe with invitation.
The square folded half,
the dream for Pythagoras
is a silken noose,
hung not-too-loose.

It begins with colour –

And the binding of grace,
threads bright-woven
heads misty-chained.

Somewhere it began –

Perhaps with sand
small-grained, deep-swept
in deserts stretched bare
under the caress of the sun,
where the hills shift and flow
with the ease of silk.

And in the song of the sand
begins the geometry of silence.

She sits on the stool.

I watched this documentary once, about honour killings in Jordan. There was this girl, whose name I don't remember now, who was stoned for talking to this guy in her village. And I remember sitting, staring at the screen, thinking, "How unbelievably barbaric, God, what an awful faith." It took me a few moments before I realised it was the same one I was born into. It was quite a shock, I can tell you. This girl was about my age, I think. And her body was left lying somewhere outside the walls of the village. It was like watching a scene from the Old Testament, courtesy of CNN.[6] And it had all the right ingredients. Black-shrouded figure lying draped on golden sand. Women wailing, men looking fierce behind big beards, young boys picking up rocks and hurling them at the cameras. You know how good Arabs are at throwing rocks.

6 **CNN:** Cable News Network, a television news channel

But who are these women? These women hidden somewhere behind layers of cloth, cloth with names like chador,[7] *abaaya*,[8] burkha, or, as Oprah says, "buuuuurker".

I have grown up watching my aunts carefully co-ordinate their outfits with their scarves. They pick them out with a sense of colour and pleasure and pride. An embroidered flower, a long fringed tassel. A clip to hold your hair in place; or nothing, so that the fabric rests in easy folds around your shoulders. The scarf is part of me, whether I accept or reject it.

So I sit and I watch this documentary, and I can't work out what I feel. Sick, mostly. Because this woman is my sister. I am linked to her in ways I don't even understand. So now, what happens to me? I get defensive. I hate what happened to this girl in Jordan. And I hate what is going to happen to women who wear scarves after people have watched the documentary. It happens all the time.

People see a woman wearing a scarf, they think "Ag, shame". Or they see a man with a piece of crocheted culture on his skull and think "terrorist". It's OK, I do it too … if I see a woman in full *hijab*, eyes peering out into the world, black material making her a walking tent, you think I don't whisper "Ninja, 10 o'clock", to my friends?

It's just that the whole world has gone a bit veil crazy. Behind the Veil. At the Drop of a Veil. To Veil or Not to Veil.

And sometimes I wonder, with my love of fabric, and texture, and colour, and beauty, with my collection of scarves that I drape around my waist, or wrap around my head but like a bandana, or loop through my belt holes, or throw around my shoulders, I wonder if I don't wear one simply because I don't like what it says.

Or maybe it's because I don't want you looking at me, the way you look at them.

The lights dim and shift towards a soft focus on the table and chair. Auntie Kariema's music begins to play, and **Sara** *puts on a colourful*

7 **chador:** Farsi word for burkha, used in Iran, where the chador is almost always black in colour

8 ***abaaya*:** (Arabic) chador or burkha

kaftan[9] *and ties a black scarf around her hair – it should be knotted firmly at the base of her neck, and all her hair should be tucked neatly away.*

Auntie Kariema

Auntie Kariema *stands behind her kitchen table. Sara is "sitting" in the chair opposite her, and Kariema addresses her monologue to the girl. She does not stop moving as she speaks; she chops onions, checks on her pots and cleans as she works. Kariema is loud, affectionate, warm and bigoted.*[10] *As the scene opens, she and Sara are locked in a debate about Azra's death.*

OK, so you want to be sad about this girl. You've been talking about her now for twenty minutes now. And I have only this to say: there is always two sides. Barbaric? What's so barbaric? You telling me that this girl had no idea she was breaking the rules, running off to see that boy? So she breaks the rules and now she must get away with it? Is that what you are saying? Let me see, let me see … ha-ah … less ginger. That girl lived her whole life in that village – whole life very happy, and must I tell you what happened?

Must I tell you? Yes or no? OK. I'll tell you. *(long pause)* Radio. Don't look at me with that blank stare. I know what I'm talking about – that village gets a radio from somewhere, next thing you know, Madonna's blaring out "Justify My Love" and "Like a Virgin", and then this girl thinks she can do what she damn well pleases.

What do you mean, the lyrics is in English? Oh, because they speak Arabic? Yes, well – don't you speak about Arabic with your head uncovered – you act like it's any other language. And anyway, with those *jintoes*[11] like Madonna and Kylie and J. Lo, you don't need to understand their words, you can … can *soema*[12] just sense their sexy nonsense with the way they sing. And that other one – Shakira! That one who move her

9 ***kaftan*:** a long loose dress
10 ***bigoted*:** obstinate, intolerant, and unwilling to accept religions/opinions different from her own
11 ***jintoes*:** prostitutes
12 ***soema*:** (Cape colloquial slang for *sommer*) without any difficulty

hips so, and says it's Latin, so she can – and you trying to tell me now that girl's not Moslem? Shakira? How many Christian girls do you know called Shakira?

What? How come I know so much about them? Because I watch MTV. Oh yes! Why must your uncle pay very good money for satellite if I can't have it on twenty-four hours a day? What you think I mus' watch the whole time? *Big Brother*. Oh *Y'Allah* … *Big Brother* – those girls are so loose, and that Groshaan – his name is Faizel. Your Auntie Moerieda went to school with his mommy.

What do you mean, I must watch something to do with my culture? What do you think I am going to watch? *Eastern Mosaic*? *This* is not a Moore[13] household. You want your Indian family, you go up the road to those people your mother married into.

Ja, ja, ja … I know it's your father's family. God! You go up the road there and you wear a sari with your stomach showing, you make a mess on your hands, you watch *Monsoon Wedding* and you wave your arms about –

She breaks mid-rant to check on her pies.

Ag, no man, *Sara* man, look at the pies! I told you to keep an eye on them, and you know my sense of smell is not what it used to be!

I now used the mince from Mr Adam's in Park Road. Last time I was at Wembley, they gave me such bad service, I said to myself, "Kariema, plush interior and fancy brass handles *of te not*,[14] you are not going back there." Mind you, that is now one thing you must say about the *charras*[15] – they really know how to make money – and then they wear the gold jewellery to prove it! Haaaahahahha. Ag, I'm just making a joke, don't get so upset …

What? Are you still on about this girl? It's the middle of the fast, I have a lot of cooking to do, and you know that it's

13 **Moore:** derogatory term for Indians
14 ***of te not*:** (Afrikaans) or not
15 ***charras*:** (slang) a somewhat negative term for people of Indian origin

haraam to *fitna* in the *pwasa*.[16] We can't keep talking about this … But you listen to me: remember when you were little and I used to warn you, "Sara, if you don't wash your face at night, the *shaytaan*[17] will come and lick it clean for you"?

You remember? Now it's the same here. If you do something naughty, here on the *Dunyia*,[18] you will get punished sooner if not later. I'm not saying she should have died, only *Allah Ta'Ala* can make that choice, but do you think I went sneaking around to meet strange boys at your age? Never! Your grandfather was very strict. I would never have married anyone he didn't one hundred per cent approve of.

And now look at me, nice big house, nice big kitchen, nice big TV, lots of children – *Algamduri'Allah*,[19] I am very happy, I can't complain. Come, come. Enough is enough! It's almost *Magriep*,[20] it's almost *boeka*[21] time … go set a place for your uncle, and go tell that cousin of yours, Nazeem, that I said he better to go *Travee*[22] tonight with his daddy. *Kom, kom, af van my stoel af, weg is jy … kom, kom.*[23]

Conscious hip-hop blares out, introducing **Ayesha**. *She comes centre stage, making repeated black power salutes, wearing a red Che Guevara*[24] *T-shirt. She is a self-professed Afro-Marxist feminist,*[25] *who looks at the world through a lens of blended discourse theory that is all her own.*

Ayesha

You see this? Che … he's my man. I'm going to name my son Che. Strong, powerful name, with a real note of resistance.

---

16 **haraam to *fitna* in the *pwasa***: forbidden to gossip during the fast
17 ***shaytaan***: devil
18 ***Dunyia***: (also *Duniya*) earth or world
19 ***Algamduri'Allah***: (also *Al-Hamdo Lillah*) praise be to Allah
20 ***Magriep***: (also *Maghrib*) sunset prayers
21 ***boeka***: Cape colloquial word for "breaking fast"; it's known as *Iftaar* in Arabic
22 ***Travee***: (also *Taraweeh*) say evening prayers at mosque during Ramadan
23 ***Kom, kom, af van my stoel af, weg is jy … kom, kom***: (Afrikaans) Come, come, get off my chair, off you go … come, come.
24 ***Che Guevara***: Cuban revolutionary leader in the late 1950s, who served in Castro's ministry
25 ***Afro-Marxist feminist***: someone who has combined three ideologies or ways of thinking about the world, i.e. combining the belief that women's rights and status should be equal to that of men with the socialist economic and political ideas of Karl Marx that were later reworked by African thinkers. The playwright is gently sarcastic about such "blended theory", as Ayesha seems rather unclear on exactly what she believes.

The thing about Che is that without him, there'd be no Fidel[26] … Everyone needs a dead icon to further their cause. And Fidel is k*k cool … not a single McDonalds in Cuba … now that's really something. Where did I get it? *(pointing to T-shirt)* Ohhhh … Truworths! Cavendish![27]

Ja, I know, it's a little, you know, unsettling, but I figure as long as I wear it, with a sense of consciousness, it's OK. Plus, I never used to go anywhere without my Malcolm X[28] cap. I got it years ago, at Sergeant Peppers, just after the movie came out. Spike Lee is a king! And these two together … you can't mess with that Revolution … clothing … very sexy.

So I was walking around Truworths today and there were like a million of these T-shirts, all in different colours. But you know, there really is only one option … red. Because I'm a Marxist.

Um, a Marxist? It's by, like, Marx, and it's, like … politics … yes … and it's … that's when like everything is, you know, when everything is like fair, and equal, and – you know *(power salute)* – black! Yeah.

But Truworths … so I'm chilling out, by the door. I am about to walk over to Diesel, 'cos they're having a sale on their Dirt Campaign Clothes – ignoring Levis, 'cos I don't buy American – when I hear *them*. The hairs on the back of my neck rise in protest, and I feel this sense of irritation bubbling up, until I am about three breaths away from screaming.

Standing slightly to the left of me, hair flicking, cellphone dangling like a bladdy earring, is Shamiela Parker and the recently married Tahira Hussein. Now these girls, and all of those like them, are the bane of my existence.[29] Call me intolerant or whatever. You just take one look at them in their camel corduroy pants, pointy-toed boots and Jahan[30] denim jackets, and you know, you just know, that they believe their

26 **Fidel:** Fidel Castro, Cuban revolutionary leader in 1950s; overthrew the government and took power

27 **Cavendish:** one of the first shopping malls in Cape Town, in the middle-class suburb of Claremont

28 **Malcolm X:** civil rights leader in the USA; imprisoned in 1946, he converted to Islam and became a Muslim priest after his release from prison

29 **bane of my existence:** constant source of trouble or annoyance in my life

30 **Jahan:** clothing factory shop, selling inexpensive high-fashion jackets and jeans

ancestors came from one place and one place only: six k's west of Malaysia, and en route down here on a ship.

Now don't get me wrong. This is not some sick case of doekie[31] envy. Just because when I put on a scarf it looks like a lampshade doesn't mean I resent these girls. No, no, no! I have academic reasons for wanting to lay the smack down.[32] We have ideological differences. And they are a brand of human being that I seriously need to subvert.[33] Tahira stopped wearing a scarf to work because her boss told her to. So much for the conviction that she loves to ram down everyone's throat!

They were standing there, planning their Eid[34] outfits …

Ayesha *begins to impersonate Shamiela.*

"Omigoooood … I was totally freaked out when I saw what you were going to wear, because you know, I just thought of something … my cousin has the exact same outfit, no, I swear … Jenni Button?[35] Ja … Ja … Well, Shaheen is picking me up in his father's Beemer[36] at about seven, after we finished greeting and everything, and then we're probably going to go to Canal Walk[37] or the Waterfront."[38]

Now this, this is what kills me. You might take a look at me and assume that I am not very religious. But you would be wrong. I take Islam very seriously … Islam mixed with a little bitta Black Consciousness, Biko, Baraka, Malcolm, big up the feminist theorists Spivak and Judith Butler, and of course my personal hero, Edward Said – with a little lelelelele-Lauren Hill in the mix. So it's the end of Ramadan,[39] and I have spent a month really purging myself. Communing with my

---

31 **doekie:** little scarf
32 **lay the smack down:** say something so offensive that they wouldn't be able to look at me
33 **subvert:** weaken or undermine
34 **Eid:** Muslim festival of Eid-ul-Fitr, marking the end of the fast of Ramadan
35 **Jenni Button:** South African designer label, associated with fairly conservative and expensive Western clothing
36 **Beemer:** (slang) BMW motor car
37 **Canal Walk:** large shopping mall just outside Cape Town city centre
38 **Waterfront:** premier tourist destination and shopping mall in Cape Town, located in the old harbour area
39 **Ramadan:** month during which practising Muslims fast from sunrise to sunset for the purpose of inner reflection and devotion to God

Creator, thinking about the poor, placing myself in spaces that's set aside this month for reflection. And I'm coming up with ways to integrate this new consciousness with my lifestyle, so I keep my head wrapped when I leave the house, for respect.

And then to hear these girls with their genuine hair and slightly Eastern features – 'cos the black blood I know is passing through their veins didn't show up as well on them as it does on me – looking for all the world like Arab princesses caught somewhere in a Western consumerist time-warp, bladdy Scheherazade[40] at the mall, looking more Muslim than I do, talking about their Jenni Button suits … well, you understand my impulse to scream.

Ja, look, I can see that you think there's more to it. There was a time in my life when the personal and the political crashed together like two trains fighting for territory on an enemy track.

It was a guy … it always is. My friend Sara's cousin Nazeem. Anyway, he had one of those hectic Muslim mothers, possessive, controlling, thinks the sun shines out of her son's arse. Auntie Kariema …. Cow! So there I was, passionate about this man, and Sara assures me that he was "different". Unconventional, didn't run with the herd, played drums … I mean, people, we are not talking about a halaal[41] raver, a Cavendish-roaming Nikes-and-Spikes boy.

So we're dating, going out, endless coffees, dagga,[42] hip-hop parties … and after a few weeks and about a hundred hints, I suddenly realise that he's avoiding taking me home. He is avoiding introducing me to his mother.

So I start thinking, OK, maybe it's the way I dress, or it's my piercings, or I'm too loud. And I ask him, and he just ignores me, and I start to whine, "Nazeem, just tell me, just tell me what is it," and then I start to scream, "Nazeem, you better tell me and if you don't, I'm going to kill you", and then I start to cry – not

40 **Scheherazade:** in literature, the clever wife of King Shahriyah, notorious for killing his wives; she escaped this fate through her ability to tell him fabulous stories in instalments, a feat she kept up for a thousand and one nights

41 **halaal:** clean or permissable

42 **dagga:** marijuana; cannabis

because I'm sad, but 'cos I'm frustrated: "Why, why, why? Are you ashamed of me?" And I keep nagging, "Why, why, why, tell me!"

And then he shouts back in a rush of words that he prays he can take back for the rest of his life: "OK, OK, Ayesha, dammit it, you're right, I can't take you home because your goddam hair is so *kroes*[43] that my mother will think you're a *boesman*,[44] and never that you're Muslim. She's totally bigoted, but it doesn't matter to me, so it shouldn't matter to you, so let's just go on with our relationship without my mother … OK?"

And while my body absorbed the emotional rocks being thrown at it, my mind reeled with solutions. So I said, "Nazeem, are you telling me that you would take me home if my hair was straight?" He nodded. "Yes." And I said, "Is that a promise?" Again, a promising nod.

So the next day, I went out and bought a wig. Yes, a long, blonde wig, k*k theatrical, designed for Rapunzel.[45] I called him up, and he had promised, so he had to take me home. And I had tea with a stunned Auntie Kariema, with my blonde wig that defied description, eating her pies, saying, "*Kanala*,[46] Auntie Kariema", and an hour later, with Nazeen still chewing his lip into a blood clot, I ceremoniously broke up with him, declining the lift he offered: "No thank you, it's started to rain, *so ek en my hare gaan huis toe.*"[47]

Anyway, the next time you hear me, I'm going to be performing at my friend Jools' Word a' Mouth gig. I've been working on a little somethin', somethin', somethin' I like to call "Ms Islam".

She waves her hand as though in a beauty pageant as an R&B track plays in the background. The spotlight fades, and **Ayesha** *walks to the rail to transform into* **Tahira**. *A cold white light focuses on the table to denote an office space.*

---

43 ***kroes***: (Afrikaans) curly or wiry, often used in a derogatory way to indicate that someone is of African or coloured descent

44 ***boesman***: (Afrikaans) Bushman, often used as an insulting reference to people classified coloured under apartheid

45 **Rapunzel:** very beautiful female character in a children's fairy tale, famous for her long hair

46 ***Kanala***: (Cape colloquialism, derived from Malay) please

47 ***so ek en my hare gaan huis toe***: (Afrikaans) so me and my hair are going home

Tahira Hussein

Tahira *wears a tightly-fitted jacket and a thin scarf resting gently on her head. She carries a handbag and makes her way to the table, which is now the desk at her place of work, Talbot Travels. She is a little superficial and catty, but is fundamentally a good person. She enters her work space alternately smiling at her colleagues and rolling her eyes at the audience. When she gets to her desk, she hastily takes off her scarf and puts it in her bag, and is about to make a surreptitious*[48] *phone call when the phone rings. She answers:*

Flying High with Talbot Travel Tahira speaking how may I help you? That's right, we have a special at the moment, return to Johannesburg for R950.00, thank you for calling … bye! *(phone rings again immediately)* Flying High with Talbot Travel Tahira speaking how may I help you? No, not Tanya, Tahira. It's Arabic. Yes, very exotic[49] … to you. No, I've never been to India. Look, can I help you with something? What am I wearing? We all wear our uniforms here at Talbot Travel … Excuse me? You want me to what? Sir! Sir! I am … no, I am a married woman! I have another call waiting, will you excuse me? Thank you, goodbye. *(She puts down the phone in horror, looks around at her work colleagues in shock, then addresses the audience.)*
You have no idea how often that happens. People are so strange, and then the perverts, they call here, and when they first hear you got a Indian name, then they wanna come with their Kama Sutra[50] ideas. It's disgusting. But I just politely told him that I'm married. And it's not a lie, hey, I am married.

Here's a picture of me and my husband Rifait on our wedding day, September first – here's Rifait, and here's me, and those are our four bridesmaids, and four best men, the three little flower girls are my nieces, and the pageboy is my husband's little brother. There was about seven hundred people there. So it wasn't such a big wedding … just family, you know. Oh! Except that girl, *(She points at the photo.)* the one with her hair all out and bushy. That's one of my cousin's friends, Ayesha.

---

48 ***surreptitious:*** stealthy; hidden; trying not be noticed
49 **exotic:** unusual; from a different culture
50 **Kama Sutra:** ancient Sanskrit book on the art of love and love-making

I can't *vriet* her,[51] I saw her outside Truworths yesterday. She always look so *angry*, but you know, I think it's because she knows, man, she doesn't really belong, you know, to our community, and plus you know what I heard? I heard she takes a *dop*.[52] And I mean of course young people do that, and a lot of the boys smoke *(She mimes inhaling a joint.)* and I also take my Camel Lights time and again, but she is just so *open*, and then at the same time she runs around screaming about women and Islam.

She came running up to me in Cavendish the other day, and asked me and my friend Shamiela, Shamiela Parker, man, asked us to sign this petition about some woman in Nigeria and she was going so on and on about this other girl in Jordan. And I don't mean to be funny man, but I just don't think that now is a good time to be criticising other Muslim people … we really need to stand together. And she just works so on my nerves, and I really wish she'd just get off her moral high horse and – *(The phone rings.)* Ag, just hold on. Flying High with Talbot Travel Tahira speaking how may I help you?

OK, sure, just hold for Mr Talbot, going through … But anyway … Rifait and me, we moved in there by my in-laws' place, but we actually saving up to get a house of our own. But don't get the wrong idea. I really like my new parents, they wonderful people, but Rifait and I want to spend as much time alone together before we have our kids. And no one will miss us, because we won't move far away. There's this stunning house just two streets away from his parents that we've got our eye on man. That's why I can't really leave this job. Just hang on a second, I have to call this work agency … I am on the lookout for something new. *(She dials.)* Engaged still.

I know, you probably think that it's wrong of me to call from Mr Talbot's phone, but you don't know what happened. Just three weeks after my wedding, he called me into his office. He starts telling me that I look really well, and asking about Rifait. Made this whole big fuss about my wedding: "Hell, that food is unbelievable. And Mrs Talbot could really use a few cooking

51 **can't *vriet* her:** (slang) can't stand her; dislike her
52 ***dop*:** (Afrikaans) alcoholic drink

lessons from your mother." And then he said, "You know, as a loyal DP[53] supporter, I've always given you people the benefit of the doubt. And you know, it's true, it's now not a lot of people that would have hired an Indian girl ten years ago."

And now I'm starting to worry, I think I'm in trouble, that I did something wrong. So I ask him, but suddenly he starts talking about September 11. "You know since the New York incident, sales have really gone down here at Talbot Travels. Now I'm not saying it's your fault."

My fault? And then he says that he can't believe that I would keep wearing a scarf after all that. That the customers don't feel comfortable buying plane tickets from me. And I start laughing, because I mean, that's like really funny, man. And he gets upset with me, starts to get very stern. Talks about company policy and our uniform. And then he says really strange things, like: "Do I cut off your ear because you spend hours on the phone to all your relatives, or your hand because you are costing me? If you want to live in a country where the women are all closed up, you wouldn't even be able to work here." And then he tries to be all nice: "Come, come, my girl, it's not such a big thing, isn't it what's on the inside that counts, we all have to give and take a little."

Basically, at the end of it, he said I could either take off my scarf or go work somewhere else. I was so shocked, hey. I went home and I told Rifait what happened, and I asked him what I must do, man, and Rifait, he just said it's now not his choice, but he'll support whatever I do. You know, I have worn a scarf since I was sixteen … because I want to.

So, now I'm left holding my scarf in one hand and unemployment in the other. I think about going out into the world with my head uncovered. I think about being at work, about people not being scared to buy plane tickets from me. I think about the house just two streets away. I think about Rifait and our time alone before we have our children. I think about having no money, I think about finding a new job.

53 **DP:** Democratic Party

Look at me. It's nearly a year later. My head is uncovered at work. My scarf stuffed in my bag. So I sit, looking for a new job. What else can I do?

She begins to dial the work agency again. The lights dim and **Tahira** *gets up, removes her clothing, and stands for a moment as* **Sara**. *The stage is lit in a warm general light.*

Sara Jacobs

The days of the fast fall in fractured spaces. Your internal clock gets set to a new rhythm. Up at four, and in the half-muted darkness, the air thick and velvety, the heat of yesterday left over, you swallow down spiced beef sandwiches and drink sugary cups of tea. The lights go on in the other houses, and as you look down the street, the flick of a switch declares a religion.

In the evening, children carry plates of food back and forth between neighbouring homes, and by the time you sit down, there's so many gifts on your table, it feels as though you are eating with your whole community. And then: Eid day. And somehow, it's all so different if you are a boy. Boys hang out in groups, and go down to mosque with their fathers, while girls stay home to cook and put *meebos*[54] and sweets into cut-glass bowls.

With every handshake, the boys reseal their friendships. They get their fathers' cars on Eid day, and later that night, the Eid fashion show begins. The venue is a shopping mall, whichever one has the longest rails and the widest catwalks. My cousin Tahira once dragged me along with her and Rifait.

Light shifts into darkness. **Sara** *reclines on her stool as though she is driving a car. The lights shift from dark to red, and we can hear the intro to Tahira's R&B song playing in the background.*

In a green BMW, with a colour-coded power-steering wheel, rocking to the sounds of the latest R&B diva, a prayer dangling from the rear-view mirror. And I vowed never again.

The light snaps back to a general state.

54 ***meebos***: (Afrikaans) strips or squares of dried fruit, a traditional South African sweetmeat

This poem goes out to Rifait and all his friends – Taariq, Mo, Yusuf – and not forgetting Psycho and Malles, even though they don't know it.

She goes to her box and puts on a fez.[55]

EID DAY

Scene one: morning

We're crisply pressed and neatly ironed
our shoes tap-tapping, gleaming black,
sitting, scrubbed, earnestly fidgeting
we've woken this morning
as we have for a month
to the cries of God

Through the mouth of a holy man
sonorously[56] calling to our homes through our sleep
that prayer is better than rest
and God is Great
(all I feel is coercion[57])
his call pulls me to my father's car
where I sink into leather smells
and religious doctrine
the mosque is full
of smiles and suits
moving mannequins
and shoes cluttering the doorway.

Scene two: afternoon

Lunchtime, and today is compulsory
so are old people's kisses,
puckered lips and stale perfume.
I want to shrink from their wrinkled embraces,
but find their grip is stronger than their heartbeats

they cling to me as though
I am life, whispering

55 ***fez:*** cone-shaped, flat-topped red hat with a black tassel on top, worn by men in some Muslim countries
56 **sonorously:** producing a deep and ringing sound
57 **coercion:** being forced

toothlessly about God and goodness,
cries and questions, "eat-this-eat-that,
You-being-good? Here-take-this-money."
Tables groan, remembering a more Spartan[58] time
framed pictures of the Ka'aba and
butterflies pinned to their graves.

Auntie Farieda sits in a corner
too fat to move, and too tired to live;
Uncle Omar is holding court[59]
he has three more pains
and a new walking stick.
He is older than Moses
and more important. He spits
in a bucket and drinks his tea in a saucer.
His wife moves softly silently
she lives softly silently,
his mother nods, forming sounds of interest
while I sit in a chair
with white fringed scarves
and embroidered silk
watching my talkative mime.

Scene three: evening

Magriep and Hallelujah!
Sleek in Armani[60]
(check my shoes from Fabiani)
I've got my father's Merc
and his phone on my belt.
We used to *skit*[61] to K.C.[62]
but now it's to the Waterfront
where we'll *tawaaf* around the banisters
greeting our *brasse*[63] at every turn.

A lean at forty-five degrees

---

58 **Spartan:** with fewer luxuries; frugal
59 **holding court:** entertaining people by telling them interesting or funny things
60 **Armani:** designer-label clothing
61 ***skit*:** (Cape colloquial slang) go
62 **K.C.:** Kenilworth Centre, a somewhat downmarket Cape Town shopping mall popular with Muslim families
63 ***brasse*:** (Cape colloquial slang) literally meaning "brothers" – refers to male friends

is a double prerequisite
for my phone and the keys
to be at ultimate exposure.
A race towards the bathroom
(while maintaining my designer roll)
reveals a crowd around the mirror
on a mission to check their gel:
Slaamat my broe[64] (my hand on my heart)
where's Psycho and Malles?

I didn't get them today –
still in Rylands?[65]
Oh … more money that way

The *kinders*[66] are looking *lekker*[67]
short skirts and *nogal*[68] scarves
Jenni Button and Donna Karan[69]
gold jewellery on their arms.
Lamming it uit met my brasse[70]
The Ummah feels so strong
We style like no other
I know that I belong.

Auntie Kariema's theme song begins to play. **Sara** *changes into a more elaborate kaftan, preferably cream with embroidery, and a matching turban-style scarf. She is standing in front of the kitchen table, at the sink, about to tackle the washing up from Eid day. The lighting is warm and general, suggesting late afternoon.*

Auntie Kariema

Shoooo, it's damn hot today. For the last four years, Labarang[71] has been on such a beautiful day, and this house has been full since the morning, everyone coming to greet here by us. See … not a thing left.

---

64 ***Slaamat my broe*:** (Afrikaans/Cape Muslim slang) peace my brother
65 **Rylands:** suburb in Cape Town, previously designated as an Indian residential area under apartheid; many middle-class Muslims live there
66 ***kinders*:** (Afrikaans) children
67 ***lekker*:** (Afrikaans) cute; attractive
68 ***nogal*:** (Afrikaans) even
69 **Donna Karan:** designer-label clothing and accessories
70 ***Lamming it uit met my brasse*:** (Afrikaans/Cape Muslim slang) going around or out with my friends
71 **Labarang:** (among Cape Muslims) Eid

My family loves my cooking. That is because I now take a lot of time thinking about at least one thing that everyone will want. My husband, Fikkie, he doesn't really like fish or vegetables very much. He's more of a meat man … and why not? He works hard all day, and if we can't have the little pleasures … you know?

But my daughter, hoooo, *Y'Allah, die kind*![72] She has gone all "Mediterranean". "Mommy, you must put olives and dolmades on the table." Dolmades? I ask her, "*Wat is daai*?"[73] And then she tells me, "It's leaves" – yes, leaves! – "stuffed with rice. It's Greek." And I think, oh no! Must I now pay a lot of money to serve my family leaves? The only leaves I cook with is bay leaves and the only stuffing I do is for my roast chicken. It's my grandmother's recipe … she's from Scotland. She turned.[74]

You know, my niece was here earlier. Sara. I am very fond of her hey. But she got some strange ideas, but that's not her fault. She now went to a white school, and has been at the univarsity[75] for a long time … so she tends to be, man what's that word I am looking for?

Dis amper soos 'n Libra, *ma isie* a Libra *nie*,[76] liber … "Liberal!" Ja, whiteys is *mos* "liberals" *na*? Not that I am calling her a whitey hey, oh no … she and her friends are always running around calling themselves *(whispers)* "black".Yes, I know … and when I said to her, "*Y'Allah*, no Sara, you can't be black," – you know, the child got such straight hair, and she isn't what a person can call *(whispers)* African. *Die kind*! She look me in my eye, and then she says to me, "Auntie Kariema, we are all African." Some people, you can't make them understand the simplest thing … too much education, they don't know if they coming or going.

But this girl she was going on so about. I know I was being a *bietjie*[77] harsh, but I mean really, what is she so concerned about this girl for? The Arabs are forever catching on k*k.

---

72 ***die kind*:** (Afrikaans) this child
73 ***Wat is daai?*:** (Afrikaans) What is that?
74 **turned:** changed religions, from Christianity to Islam
75 **univarsity:** mispronunciation of university
76 ***Dis amper soos 'n* Libra, *ma isie* a Libra *nie*:** (Cape Afrikaans dialect) It's almost like a Libra, but isn't a Libra
77 ***bietjie*:** (Afrikaans) little bit

I mean don't get me wrong, I also want to go to *Makkha*[78] one day, *Insh'Allah*,[79] but those bladdy Arabs act like they own Islam. You know, you always hear these horror stories from people who have gone on haj,[80] that's the pilgrimage hey, and they say that there, the women may walk around in full *hijab* outside, but the minute they set a foot indoors … it's *net*[81] designer miniskirts! Yes, it's true! And my cousin came back now-now from Malaysia. She said over there they got a thing called "macon". *Y'Allah* … spice beef made to taste like bacon … macon! Well, I am sorry, but that is just one letter away from haraam as far as I am concerned. And we have a name for people like that here … *water slamse.*[82]

Oooh, I mustn't talk like this, *Y'Allah* forgive me, Fikkie gets so upset, but it really irritates me. They come down here, and they expect everyone must make a big bladdy fuss, and *skielik*[83] no one is saying "*tramakasie*"[84] or "*kanala*" anymore. Oh no, it's now "*shukran*"[85] and "*afwan*".[86] *Shukran* – I mean, what is that? My mother taught me to say *tramakasie*, so *tramakasie* is what I'll say. Mind you, it's not just the Arabs hey … it's the *charras* also. They have a bladdy field day with Arabic – when they not saying "jee this" and "jee that". And must I tell you something for nothing very quick? They now *nogal* not here all that long. They all came one, maybe two generations ago, but we Malays have been here for over three hundred years. And let me tell you something about us, we may have lost our language, but we have never lost our *dien*.[87] And we may be stuck here at the bottom of Africa, but we know where we come from.

But *Jirre*,[88] about this girl. Sara kept on and on at me, about how it's unfair, it's unfair, it's unfair. Well you know what? Life is unfair.

---

78 ***Makkha***: Mecca, in Saudi Arabia, holiest city in the Muslim world
79 ***Insh'Allah***: God willing
80 **haj:** pilgrimage to Mecca, which all Muslims are expected to make at least once
81 ***net***: (Afrikaans) only
82 ***water slamse***: (Cape colloquial) those whose Islamic faith is "watered down"
83 ***skielik***: (Afrikaans) suddenly
84 ***tramakasie***: (derived from Malay) thank you
85 ***shukran***: (Arabic) thank you
86 ***afwan***: (Arabic) you're welcome – said in response to *shukran*
87 ***dien***: (also *deen*) religion or faith
88 ***Jirre***: (Cape colloquial slang) God; Lord

My mother got married when she was sixteen. My father was forty. Ag, it wasn't so unusual back then. And they settled down together and they had six children. Me, my brothers Mustapha and Ridwaan, and my sisters, Fatima, Shami, and Farieda. Anyway, my mother and I were very close. From whence I was small already, I'd sit at this wooden table in the kitchen and watch her, how she makes the pies.

Wag nou, wag nou, ek sal vir julle nou wys …[89] *(She gets up and begins to demonstrate.)* First you measure out your flour and your butter. Then, you sift your flour, then you delicately rub your flour in with your butter. *En* butter, *hoor*! *Nie* Marvelo *nie*![90] You delicately rub your flour in with your butter. *En* delicate, *hoor*! *Ons maak nie* cement *nie*![91] Then you roll out your dough, and you wrap him in the cling wrap, and you put him in the fridge, he must settle. Ooooh, and the pots would be simmering with these wonderful smells of mince or chicken mixed with onions and cloves and garlic, and my mother's beautiful face would be flushed from the steam.

And she always smiled while she cooked, because later, she said, people who ate your food would taste your happiness.

As she reminisces,[92] *she is struck by a memory that saddens her deeply. She begins to confide in the audience.*

My mother died when I was ten. For five months she lay in a bed, wasting away slowly, while doctor did what he could. My father was in the background somewhere … he couldn't make sense of it … she was so young, he was much older, but still healthy.

And the day of her funeral was dark, hey. It was so strange … it was dark, but it wasn't cold. Just dark and grey. My aunties were all there, crying. That same day, they, the *tukamanies,*[93] took her into a room. I knew that they were going to wash her and prepare her for burial, but I just couldn't go in. Maybe I

---

89 ***Wag nou, wag nou, ek sal vir julle nou wys …*:** (Afrikaans) Wait, wait, I'll show you now …

90 ***En* butter, *hoor*! *Nie* Marvelo *nie*!:** (Afrikaans) And be sure to use butter, and not Marvelo margarine!

91 ***Ons maak nie* cement *nie*!:** (Afrikaans) We are not making cement!

92 ***reminisces*:** thinks back with fondness

93 ***tukamanies*:** people who prepare the body for Muslim burial

should have … but the thought of my mother, lying naked, and dead in that big tin washtub, with other people's hands sponging her body … however lovingly … was now too much for me, man.

So I stayed in the kitchen, sitting near the stove, where it was warm, not really wanting to move or think. But maybe I should have gone into that room, because later, when she was wrapped in white sheets, pressed with camphor and rose petals, and lifted above the men's shoulders, ready to be taken to the *koebus*,[94] I don't know what made me think I could go with them. But I followed the men out the door, and tried to tag along, maybe make myself unnoticed … because you see, I needed to bury my mother.

And one of the men, a stranger who walked close by the coffin, turned to me and said, "What are you doing? You know you're not allowed, go back to the house." But you see, I kept on walking, because I needed to bury my mother. I kept walking until my father, his face full of pain, picked me up and carried me to the stoep[95] by our house. I stood there crying, while the women went inside to make pies and tea and sandwiches with their grief.

Auntie Kariema *searches for her cigarettes and, finding them, sits down heavily and lights up, drawing deeply.*

So this girl, this Arab girl. I suppose I can understand her … I wanted to walk, she wanted to talk.

The light holds her for a long moment; she exhales, and it dims. **Kariema** *changes into* **Tahira**'s *costume; a longish Indian top, and a matching scarf that hangs around her neck.*

Tahira Hussein

As **Tahira** *turns, we see that she is heavily pregnant. She is speaking animatedly*[96] *on her cellphone. She pulls the chair into the centre of the stage. At different points in her monologue she gets up, moves the chair, massages the small of her back, and stretches.*

94 ***koebus*:** grave or graveyard
95 **stoep:** front verandah of a house
96 ***animatedly*:** using vigorous gestures

... No Rifait, you still my baby. Now? I'm just getting the new room ready. No, I won't move anything heavy. OK, OK, salaam.[97] *(She sits down.)*

I know! Can you believe it? It's a girl. I just asked the gynae. And I was so relieved it was a girl because Rifait said if it was a boy, then he wanted to name him after his father, but his daddy's name is Adam. And I don't mean to be funny *nê*, but I really don't think that now is the right time to be calling my son Adam Hussein!

You know I had to now work at Talbot Travel for three months before I realised I was expecting, and Rifait said I must leave because it was just stressing me out, and it wasn't good for the baby. And I was glad to leave, but it meant that we couldn't get that house that we were saving up for, man.

But you know, it has really meant time out for me to do my own thing. You remember my friends Nasreen and Shamiela? They were here now the other day, they threw me this baby shower, and my cousin Sara was there with that Ayesha girl, she was so in my face the whole time: "Why don't you call the baby Che? Why don't you call the baby Che?" And I just thought to myself, mhpfffff, she didn't even have the decency to bring my baby a present, but she wants to give my baby a name? I don't think so!

You should have seen the presents my family bought me. My *nani*[98] sent me these stunning little gold bangles all the way from Jo'burg. Ja, and anyway, you know Nasreen was there in these cool new Nine West[99] boots, she was just showing them so off the whole time, and I just had to smile, 'cos there's no way that these ankles are getting into those boots for the next few months. So I am at home a lot, and this has really meant that I have a lot of time to bond with my mother-in-law. *(She pulls a face indicating she can't stand her mother-in-law, and then gets up to check if she can hear her.)* I mean she really is a wonderful person ... but she just works so on my nerves!

---

97 **salaam:** Muslim greeting, literally meaning "peace"
98 ***nani*:** granny (mother's mother)
99 **Nine West:** upmarket shoe store

You know, she is always coming through our separate entrance, she walks through my kitchen, she looks in my pots, she looks in my cupboards, she even goes through Rifait's washing, and I think she always did it, but now I am around to see it! You know the other day we had this huge fight because I was making dhal[100] for Rifait. And you know, my mother taught me a different recipe. And then his mommy tried to come with extra dhania,[101] less chilli, telling me my garam masala[102] was wrong, urrrrrggggh!

I just got so cross, I said, "He's my husband, I know what he likes." And then she put her hand on my stomach like this and said, "One day when you have a son of your own, you will also realise that a mother always knows what's best."

Sometimes I can get quite lonely. But I read a lot, and I watch TV, and I go shopping. You know the other day I was in Woolworths, I was buying some steak for Rifait for supper … no, no, the new Woolworths in Cavendish has a halaal section, so I only buy my meat there, and I was standing there, trying to decide now what steak, when I just heard this voice behind me: "I wouldn't trust that if I were you … why don't you buy from Mr Adams?"

And I turned around and I saw that it was Sara's auntie, Auntie Kariema … you know some people are just so *bus*![103] And she asked me about the baby, started telling me that ginger was good for nausea, and about how her son Nazeem was doing so well at law school, and I was trying to find a way to like make a break for it, so I just picked up the first paper I could, and I saw something on the front page that totally shocked me.

It was a picture of this Iraqi baby. Her face was so perfect, she was like a little doll, with tiny eyes squeezed shut, and a little nose. She must have been about three months.

And I'm looking at this picture and I'm thinking no man, there's something wrong here, and that's when I saw that her head was covered in blood. And even though she had a little

100 **dhal:** spicy pea or lentil dish
101 **dhania:** Indian term for coriander
102 **garam masala:** Indian spice blend (cooks often mix their own blend)
103 ***bus*:** (Cape colloquial slang) nosy

scarf or bandage wrapped round her head, the blood was everywhere, it seeped right though the cloth.

And then I saw something that made me feel like I lost my breath … the dummy was still in the mouth.

And everyone in the queue is talking about this picture, and this man says, "Ja, well … that's the price you pay for terrorism!" And I just politely turned around to him and said, "Does that baby look like a terrorist to you?"

Anyway, I went home, and I spent a long time, just sitting, just like this. You know, sometimes I get so scared to bring our baby into all this. You know, the longer I carry her, the more I understand what it takes to help another person into this world. Sometimes I lie awake at night, and I swear I can hear her heartbeat inside me. I thought about the baby in that picture, and I just prayed that her mother wasn't alive to see it.

Tahira *sits on the chair in silence. The light dims and she removes her costume, once again becoming* **Sara**. *Sara moves energetically across the stage, and as she begins to speak, she removes the hanging scarf from its hooks.*

Sara Jacobs

Madressa. Three o'clock. And the boredom is palpable. We would say that even the flies were too tired to move, trapped in the folds of those curtains that never opened.

She drapes the scarf over her head.

Every day after school, we would walk, my sister and I, our white or cream burkhas that hid our brightly coloured T-shirts, to Sheik Hussein's Muslim school. He was a scholarly man with a little beard, piercing black eyes, and a fez perched jauntily on his head. He had an Indian accent, a long, smooth wooden stick he used to point out suras,[104] and a way of moving his head while he recited that was hypnotising.

Those afternoons spent at Madressa exist somewhere in a haze of learning and submission. When we all bent over to

104 **suras:** (also *surahs*) chapters of the Qu'ran

learn how to *salaat*,[105] my most poignant[106] memory is of my best friend whispering:

She places the scarf on the ground like a prayer mat, kneels on it and bends over, whispering loudly while pretending to pray:

"Jy! Jy! Do you have a bubblegum for me? No? Shafiek … do you have a bubblegum?"

And then later, we would sit at a long rectangular wooden table, about thirty boys and girls. Our heads bent over texts written in a fluid, organic writing, the same writing that hung in gold letters around our homes, around our necks, in our cars. We sounded out words in Arabic, the language of the East, of faraway countries, of deserts and camels, and somehow home, never fully understanding what we read. But the recitation would stir something in us that went beyond language.

The same understanding that was breathed into our ears by our fathers on the day we were born. The *shahaddah*:[107] The declaration of faith, pivotal to our lives – *(She recites in Arabic first.)* "There is no God but God, and Mohamed is his Messenger."

How many ways has it changed for me? When I first heard it in a world that wasn't yet sound-tracked by doubt and questioning, did it sound any different?

And the answer I get, or the answer I am told is … no. It never changes. It never shifts. It is a truth. Its existence, its eternity, its reality is not up for discussion … And I start to think, I don't believe … I don't believe that any of that depends on making sure I wear this. *(She holds up a scarf.)*

While **Sara** *holds the scarf out as a challenge, conscious hip-hop blares out again, introducing* **Ayesha**. *She comes forward, and the music stops. She is wearing a mid-length skirt over pants, and her head is covered by a long length of material wrapped as a turban. A spotlight comes up, as does the music for her poem.*

---

105 ***salaat*:** pray
106 **poignant:** evoking a keen sense of sadness or regret
107 ***shahaddah*:** affirmation of faith by Muslims

In the slam poem[108] performance piece that follows, Ayesha recites against the backdrop of a musical score. The first verses, before the refrain "So, so, so ..." are set against a soothing rhythmic acid jazz beat, while the verses that follow are performed in an angry, confrontational hip-hop mode.

The poem reveals a more feminine and wounded side of her character. She speaks and sings over the beats in the background.

Ayesha

Good evening, my brothers and sisters. My name is Ayesha, and I am here tonight to present to you my words. This is called "Ms Islam".

I'm here to tell a story tonight
beginning somewhere, beyond the earth,
in a sky turned white
before God thought that life would be worth-
while to breathe light into it.
We begin with souls
at the core of the Qu'ran
existing in a space, far before man
dwelling in voids that knew no gender
who would have thought that physical bodies would
render them apart
apart, apart, apart.

So if that's the start
is this the ending?
Where laws are made
and there is no bending?
No, no, no, there is no bending

Where are all these women
that I feel around me every day?
They live in words and whispers
my global Ummah sisters.
What about Ayesha, the prophet's wife?
She translated shari'ah[109] law in her life

108 ***slam poem:*** poetry that carries a very strong criticism
109 **shari'ah:** sacred law of Islam

a scholar, a warrior, a poet, a passion
universal woman before the medieval fashion.

Sometimes I get angry –
trapped inside my head
can't make sense of the voices
woven into thread
that should be wrapped around my dread
locks
Standing here staring down at my feet
knowing that's where my children will meet
Paradise
I devise

That what I see is journeys
maps made of silk
and routes of freedom that have not yet been built
And routes to freedom that have not yet been built.

So, so, so, so, so … *(tempo changes)*

To my sisters in Afghanistan
dodging beatings from the Taliban
trying to make sense of a US marshal
who thinks it's OK, it's OK to drop a bomb a bomb
and then a food parcel

To my sisters in Palestine
in the camps doing prison time
locked in the rubble of Jenin
which is a docu-makers dream
I mean
nightmare

To my sisters in Baghdad, Basra, Iraq
baby girl, lying dead, dummy still in her mouth
oil is burning, tenders[110] made
they say they rebuild a nation
this looks like occupation
not liberation

To my sister in Nigeria

110 **tenders**: formal written offers to carry out work or supply goods

facing death from the shari'ah
why should she suffer Azra's fate
for "God-forbid" choosing, choosing,
choosing her own mate?

To my sisters in history, in Cape Town's past
trapped, attached to the slave, the slave-ship's mast
Saartjie van die Kaap[111] and Cissie Gool[112]
Muslim women who redefined the rules
my sisters in the frontline of the UDF
when scarves were a way of saying "voetsek"[113] –

Know that I make it my business not to forget.

No I won't forget,
my routes to freedom,
that have not yet been built
and my sisters, my global Ummah sisters
where my roots, where my roots?
And where are my sisters?

The lights fade to a complete blackout. The strains of tabla music are heard once again. **Ayesha** *changes into* **Azra's mother**, *who wears a simple black cotton shift and a large patterned scarf.*

Azra's mother

Azra's mother *navigates her way gently about the stage in a series of dance-like movements, using a large scarf to accentuate[114] her gestures. She eventually moves centre upstage. Blue lights come up as she makes her way towards her daughter. When she gets there, and sits down, the lights change to red. She sits on the stage, holding Azra's head in her lap.*

Your name is Azra, and you are my daughter. The al Jamal, the part of you your father claimed, is gone now. Drifting through endless grains of sand that now house your blood. I am sitting here, holding your head softly in my lap, near to the place that I pushed you from me years ago. When I first saw you, covered

111 **Saartjie van die Kaap:** Sarah of the Cape; a freed slave woman, who was the first Muslim (and black) woman to own property in the Cape, which she then donated as land on which to build a mosque
112 **Cissie Gool:** one of the first female Muslim political activists in the struggle against apartheid
113 **voetsek:** (an exclamation) get lost; go away
114 **accentuate:** make more noticeable

Azra's mother (Quanita Adams) mourns her daughter's death.

in blood and out of my womb where I had kept you secret and safe for all those months, I reached out and wept that you were born a girl. Not because I wanted a son. People often think that a mother's desire for a son is to please her husband. Not so. We don't want girls because we don't want our children to be prisoners of their own bodies.

Wrapped in cloth that hides you from the world the minute you start to bleed. The minute your body begins to speak of its power and its capabilities. Wrapped, hidden.

I hold you in a circle of gentleness and a flood of tears. There are no words. No words for you, or your life that didn't happen, or the senselessness of your death. No words for the men that have lost their humanity and their connection to God through your murder. You are mine again, as I hold you close to me in an embrace of blood, so like your beginning. You are somewhere in the Gardens of God. I know that. Somewhere with hills flushed green and water sparkling in rivers of transparent sweetness. You are in the arms of the Most Merciful, and at the feet of the Infinitely Compassionate. And I, I am your mother, and I send you greetings of peace. I am the mother of memory and I will bear witness. I will not forget.

The end

Questions and activities

Pre-reading activities

Learners should make a few notes during and after each of these pre-reading activities, either individually, in groups, or as a class. It will be useful to refer to their ideas and feelings as they are now, and as they are during and after reading and discussing the play.

1 All learners (both girls and boys) cover your heads with a scarf, putting it over your heads and covering your faces. Discuss the following: How easy is it to put on and keep on? How does it make you feel? What is it like to have your face covered with a thin cloth that you can see through? (Note: In the burkha there may be a thinner mesh section to look through.) How do others look, covered this way? Why do you think women through the ages have been veiled? For what reasons are brides sometimes still veiled?

2 Are there certain ways of dressing in your culture or religion? If so, when do you dress this way and why? If there is no specific way of dress, can you say why not? Has it always been this way, or have some things changed over the years?

3 In your community, are there certain ways in which men and women are expected to relate to one another? Do you agree with these rules, or could they be changed in some way? Do you feel free to discuss male and female roles and rules, or are you not really allowed or supposed to? How do you feel about this? Do the boys and girls in the class see such issues in the same way?

4 Do all of you in the class come from similar backgrounds in terms of culture, tradition, and religion? Don't assume that you know all about each other – ask questions. Even within one religious faith there may be a variety of styles of worship. Between religions there may be similarities you are unaware of – you will discuss this at a later stage.

5 Discuss Islam in particular and pool your knowledge about this religion. Be careful not to confuse fact with hearsay or assumption. Discuss ways in which you can check your facts.

6 Look up the meaning of these words from the themes of the play: prejudice; bias; discrimination. Discuss how these terms are related to one another.

Quiz

After an initial reading of the play, use this quiz to assess your understanding of key elements of the setting, characters, plot, and themes. Assessment: informal (peer marking).

Multiple choice

Choose the correct option to complete each sentence.

1 Azra's family kills her because
A they don't like her
B they want to restore their honour
C they don't like the man she wants to marry
D she won't wear a scarf. (1)

2 "*Charra*" is a slang term for
A a dog
B a cleaner
C a Muslim child
D an Indian. (1)

3 Sara is Auntie Kariema's
A cousin
B niece
C daughter
D daughter-in-law. (1)

4 Rifait is Tahira's
A husband
B brother
C boyfriend
D father. (1)

5 Tahira resigns because
   A she hates her job
   B she is harassed
   C she is pregnant
   D she doesn't need the money. (1)

6 One of Ayesha's political heroes is
   A Karl Marx
   B Che Guevara
   C Nelson Mandela
   D Spike Lee. (1)

Other questions

7 In which city is the play set? (1)
8 Around which religion is the play centred? (1)
9 Although the play is in English, vocabulary from three other languages is also used. Name the three languages. (3)
10 Name the state that Azra comes from. (1)
11 Why won't Ayesha's boyfriend take her to meet his mother? (2)
12 Why were Sikh men harassed and attacked after the September 11 terrorist attacks? (2)
13 State which of the following is the *main* theme of this play, giving a reason for your choice: gender bias; racism; tradition; South African culture. (2)
14 Does the play end on a negative or positive note? Quote to support your answer. (Note: this is not the same as sad or happy – think about the difference before answering.) (2)

Short questions

Use these short questions to guide your reading and discussion of the play.

Monologue 1: Azra al Jamal (pages 21–22)

First Additional Language (FAL)

1 As you read, how can you tell the difference between stage directions and what the characters say? Name two things. (2)
2 The stage directions describe a number of elements of drama, the first one being "props" (furniture and other

things used by the actors). List the other elements described here. (4)

3 Describe what Azra is wearing in this scene (you may need to find pictures to help you). (2)

Home Language (HL)

1 Draw a plan (bird's-eye view) of the stage for this scene, showing where the props are placed. (6)

2 Read the scene, and then decide how the lighting might change as the blue light fades at the beginning. Factors such as the time of day and the mood (feelings) should be taken into account. (3)

3 State briefly two main themes introduced here. (2)

4 Although she gives a graphic description of her own death, Azra's monologue is not simply harshly realistic. Identify two elements of her speech that are not realistic in style. Look for figurative language (imagery, comparisons), choice of adjectives and adverbs, repetition, and other devices. (4)

All levels, including Drama Studies

Write your own personal response to this scene, using descriptive adjectives and comparisons to communicate your feelings. Keep your writing and refer back to it once you have studied the whole play. (no assessment)

Monologue 2: Sara Jacobs (pages 22–25)

First Additional Language

1 Refer to the poem "The Scarf" and briefly explain the references to Egypt and Pythagoras. (3)

2 a What explanation does this poem give for why scarves are worn? (2)

b Identify the linked themes that are being discussed. (2)

3 Using your dictionary and thesaurus, as well as class discussion, find at least two adjectives to describe someone like Sara who thinks about issues and tries not to take sides. (2)

Home Language

1 Refer to the poem "The Scarf".

a State the reason Sara gives for the scarf being worn. (1)

   b Does she support this reason? Justify your answer. (3)

2 a Outline the connotations of the words "noose" and "chained". (2)

   b Identify the theme they explore and outline how they do so. (3)

3 Quote the line where Sara pokes fun at a Western stereotype of Arabs. (1)

Acting it out

The stage directions say Sara takes time to choose a scarf with which to recite her poem. Discuss and rehearse this, exploring options such as these: Does she find one soon? Does she take different scarves at different points in the poem? Does she keep a scarf in her hands while she sits and talks about Azra? Does she get up again at any point? Make sure your movements are motivated by the character's words or internal thoughts.

Monologue 3: Auntie Kariema (pages 26–28)

First Additional Language

1 To whom is Auntie Kariema talking, and what are they talking about? (2)

2 Quote an expression used here that is typically South African. (1)

3 Why does Auntie Kariema feel she can criticise Sara's family, when they are surely her family too? (2)

4 List at least two prejudices or stereotypes that Auntie Kariema has about Indian people. (2)

5 What is the purpose of this character, in terms of the themes of the play? (3)

Home Language

1 Examine the stage directions and Auntie Kariema's style of speech and identify two ways in which the playwright creates a very active character. (2)

2 a Explain what is ironic about Auntie Kariema's criticism of Western music and singers. (2)

   b How does she justify this contradiction? (2)

3 In what way does the playwright explore her themes through this character? (4)

Acting it out

Is Auntie Kariema's cooking all mimed? How many props would you use/allow? You will need to discuss various options and then try them out – borrow pots and kitchen tools from the Consumer Studies department.

Monologue 4: Ayesha (pages 28–32)

First Additional Language

1 Ayesha uses typical conversational expressions such as "like" and "you know". How does this help the audience to identify with her character? (2)

2 There is clearly conflict between Ayesha and the two girls she describes. Draw up a table like the one here. Fill in how the girls see each other (through Ayesha's eyes, at this point), and what theme this expresses (you may want to add to this later, after reading Monologue 5). (6)

Example:

Tahira and Shamiela	Ayesha	Theme
They think Ayesha: • does not look Muslim •	She thinks they: • are snobbish about their Malay ancestry •	• Prejudices about culture •

Home Language

1 Explain why Ayesha makes so many references to what the other girls wear. (4)

2 a Identify the metaphorical link between Ayesha and Azra, in the term "emotional rocks". (2)

b How do their situations allow them to react differently? (4)

Acting it out

- Find a picture of Che Guevara and create a design that would be suitable for printing onto a T-shirt.
- Define at least two ways in which Ayesha and Shamiela would move or gesture differently and then act out Ayesha's impersonation of Shamiela and her subsequent comments.

Monologue 5: Tahira Hussein (pages 33–36)

First Additional Language

1 Like several characters in the play, Tahira seems to have double standards. Give one example of this. (2)

2 "I've always given you people the benefit of the doubt," Mr Talbot tells Tahira. Identify the prejudice that is subtly expressed in the words "you people". (2)

3 Do you think Mr Talbot is justified in asking Tahira to remove her scarf at work? Give two reasons for your answer. If you can't decide, give one reason on each side of the argument. (3)

Home Language

1 Like several characters in the play, Tahira seems to have double standards. Identify one example of this and comment on whether you find any such double standards in your own life, or in those around you. (2)

2 "I've always given you people the benefit of the doubt," Mr Talbot tells Tahira. What theme is subtly addressed here? Justify your answer. (2)

3 a According to Tahira, how has Mr Talbot justified his request that she remove her scarf at work? (2)

b What argument could you use to oppose his view? (2)

Acting it out

Either script and enact, or improvise one of the following conversations:

- Tahira and her husband discuss her wearing the scarf at work.
- Two of Tahira's work colleagues share their opinions after overhearing Mr Talbot's remarks to Tahira.
- Mr Talbot relates his "problems" at work to his wife.

Monologue 6: Sara Jacobs (pages 36–39)

First Additional Language

1 Explain how "the flick of a switch declares a religion". (2)

2 Find one positive point and one negative point about the fast, in the second paragraph. (2)

3 Briefly summarise the activities in the three periods of the day that mark Eid day. (3)

Home Language

1 Note two examples of poetic language in the first paragraph of this monologue and comment on how this language reflects Sara's character. (3)

2 Like Ayesha earlier, Sara dislikes the consumerism of many young Muslims. Refer back to Ayesha's monologue about Ramadan to find the religious reason for both girls' disapproval. (3)

3 In many ways the Eid day is like festival days in any community. What two things remind us, in scene two of the Eid day poem, that this is a Muslim community? (2)

Acting it out

Discuss how you would move while saying the poem "Eid Day". Consider these points: How much would you mime or re-enact? Where and when would you move – only between each scene, or more often? In class you could act out the three scenes described in the poem, taking on the characters of fathers, uncles, aunts, friends, and so on.

Monologue 7: Auntie Kariema (pages 39–43)

First Additional Language

1 In what way is the content of Auntie Kariema's monologue typical of many mothers? (3)

2 Identify the political stereotype Auntie Kariema applies. (2)

3 Reread from "*Dis amper soos 'n* Libra ..." to "... they don't know if they coming or going". What prejudice does Auntie Kariema reveal in these two paragraphs? (1)

4 According to Muslim law, women are not allowed to attend funerals. How does Auntie Kariema's memory of her mother's funeral enable her to identify with Azra, the Jordanian girl? Quote one line to support your answer. (4)

Home Language

1 Auntie Kariema has several things to say about "Arabs". Make a list of her prejudices against them. (3)

2 In Auntie Kariema's closing line, we see her find new sympathy for "this Arab girl".

a Identify the similarity between Auntie Kariema and Azra. (1)

b Explain what Auntie Kariema is referring to when she says, "I wanted to walk, she wanted to talk". (2)

c Comment on how this statement links to a theme of the play. (3)

3 Auntie Kariema smokes at the end of this monologue. Why has the playwright specifically included this action? By way of explanation, discuss Auntie Kariema's character and how she feels at this moment. (3)

Acting it out

- Consider the part where Auntie Kariema does the washing up. Would you use real props to some extent, or just mime this?
- Identify the movements you could use to suggest the hot day – for example, wiping your forehead.
- The breaks in the script tell you when to pause because the emotion changes – for example, after "... life is unfair" (pages 41–43). Plan how long these pauses would be, and whether any movement would accompany them.

Monologue 8: Tahira Hussein (pages 43–46)

First Additional Language

1 a State briefly why Tahira has stopped working. (1)

b Give one positive and one negative consequence of this. (2)

2 In what way is Tahira's relationship with her mother-in-law rather typical or stereotyped? (2)

3 a Describe the picture Tahira sees in the newspaper. (2)

b Give one reason why it upsets her. (1)

Home Language

1 a Name one way in which Tahira's mother-in-law fits the stereotype. (1)

b Explain how the stereotyped mother-in-law adds humour and arouses empathy for Tahira. (3)

2 When Tahira sees the picture in the newspaper, a man in the queue comments on it. From the man's comments, say briefly how the baby might have been killed and by whom (refer to the notes on September 11 if necessary). (3)

Acting it out

Discuss whether or not this is a point at which you could use multi-media such as projected images of the incident to which Tahira refers. Would it help to show the picture of a baby, such as she describes? Would you enact and record the scene at the shop, and show it here, rather than just have Tahira speak about it?

Monologue 9: Sara Jacobs (pages 46–47)

First Additional Language

1 Was the young Sara's time at Sheik Hussein's school completely meaningless? Quote three consecutive words to support your answer. (2)

2 In Sara's opinion, what is the connection between the truth of Islam, and the wearing of a scarf? (2)

Home Language

1 Sara's description of her time at Sheik Hussein's school is very specific, with many religious references. How is a non-Muslim audience member still able to identify with her experience? (2)

2 Sara mentions the "declaration of faith" learnt at Islamic school. Explain what her final sentence ("And I start to think …") says about her understanding of this truth. (3)

Acting it out

How do you attract someone's attention without the teacher noticing? Get down on the floor with a partner, like Sara and her friend, and find gestures and movements that are visible to your friend and the audience, but not to an imaginary teacher!

Monologue 10: Ayesha (pages 48–50)

First Additional Language

1 State the main themes of the play that are reflected and summarised in this poem. (3)

2 "… that's where my children will meet/Paradise …" (stanza 4). Quote the play's *opening* reference to Paradise that this links to. (1)

Home Language

1 Poetic devices used in the poem include repetition, rhyme, rhythm, and a play on words. Identify two of these devices and explain their effect. (4)

2 In the first part of the poem, Ayesha mentions five issues: the divisions that gender brings; unbending laws; the sisterhood of Islam; her own questions; ways to freedom. Write down each of these points and, next to each one, write down a relevant quote from the poem to support the issue. (5)

3 Outline how Sara's monologue prepares us for the issues raised here by Ayesha and how Ayesha's monologue picks up on Sara's. (4)

Acting it out

Discuss ways in which you could support the text with movements and gestures. You might first need to agree on the pace of the poem in each section. Would it be possible to present the poem in a group, dividing the sections between both individual and grouped voices? Try out several options.

Monologue 11: Azra's mother (pages 50–51)

First Additional Language

1 Reread the stage directions for Azra's mother (page 50), and those for her daughter in the opening scene of the play (page 21). List the directions for movement and lighting for each scene. (4)

2 a In what way do the mother's words echo the play's opening Hadith? (1)

b Explain why one could say that the play ends on a positive or reassuring note. (2)

Home Language

1 State one similarity and one difference between the stage directions for Azra's mother, and those for her daughter in the opening scene of the play. (2)

2 Comment on the theatrical effect of the mother cradling her daughter's head in her lap. (Note: this is imaginary – there is only one actress.) (2)

3 In what way could one say that Azra's mother reveals power, despite her veiled life? (3)

Acting it out

How would you show the audience that it is your daughter you are holding? Walk through the actions from the time when Azra's mother reaches her daughter, to when she actually sits down. How does she lift her head? Could you use an extra scarf in some way here? It might help to have someone actually lying there, so you can feel the action; and to have a few act it out, while others watch and comment and learn. Remember also that, although you are speaking "down" to your lap, you need to address the audience. On your own, select places where you could look down at your daughter. Where else would you look?

Paragraph questions

Paragraph questions can be marked out of 10–15 marks, and the answers are usually around 80–150 words long. Check the latest Subject Assessment Guidelines (SAG) for exam requirements.

Monologue 1: Azra al Jamal (pages 21–22)

1 (FAL and HL) Explain how the opening monologue generates (gives rise to) the subsequent monologues and, to some extent, the structure of the play.

Monologue 2: Sara Jacobs (pages 22–25)

2 (FAL) Explain as briefly as possible the references to "terrorist" and "veil crazy", using the notes on September 11 on pages 75–76 to help you.

3 (HL) The character of Sara is thoughtful and reflective. Responding to the stoning, she is first "sick", then defensive, then questions her own reasons for not wearing a scarf. Explain each of these reactions in turn, and link each to a theme or themes.

Monologue 3: Auntie Kariema (pages 26–28)

4 (FAL and HL) Choose one prejudice voiced by Auntie Kariema and explain her views, and why they may be termed bigoted or prejudiced.

Monologue 4: Ayesha (pages 28–32)

5 (FAL and HL) Describe the difference in looks between Ayesha and the other girls. How does this relate to their culture and religion?

Monologue 5: Tahira Hussein (pages 33–36)

6 (FAL and HL) Now that you have "met" the South African women in the play, choose one and write a paragraph in which you compare her to someone you know who is quite like her.

Monologue 10: Ayesha (pages 48–50)

7 "… it's quite clear that if one of the women in the play who is not Middle Eastern was stoned to death, the reaction would be very different … there should not be double standards of freedom for here and the women over there …" (interview with Nadia Davids on pages 12–17). How does Ayesha's poem lead us towards this understanding? Refer in particular to the various "sisters" she mentions, and the order in which they appear.

Essay questions

These questions can be used for FAL and HL learners. FAL learners should write an essay of 150–200 words (Grade 10), 200–250 words (Grade 11), or 250–300 words (Grade 12) for 35 marks. HL learners should write an essay of 300–350 words (Grade 10), 350–400 words (Grade 11), or 400–450 words (Grade 12) for 25 marks. Teachers should consult the Subject Assessment Guidelines for further information.

1 Choose the character with whom you most strongly identify in the play. Analyse this character in terms of her dialogue and action, and how these relate to the themes of the play. Conclude with an explanation of how strongly you identify with her, and why.

2 Explain the structure of the play and how this relates to the plot and themes. You should mention ways in which the play is typical or unusual in terms of both structure and plot.

3 Trace the theme of gender bias as it is expressed in the scarf. Include both literal and figurative references, as well as design elements such as movement and costume.

4 Discuss the roles of the various men mentioned or portrayed in the play and how they form part of the plot and themes.

5 Divide into three or six groups to discuss the poems "The Scarf", "Eid Day" and "Ms Islam" (one poem per group). Consider the following: structure (verses, rhyme, line length); emotions; figurative language; poetic devices such as repetition. Once each group has analysed its poem, tell the class about it and then draw some general conclusions about the use of poetry in the play as a whole. Individually, learners summarise their conclusions in an essay.

Topics for discussion

Monologue 2: Sara Jacobs (pages 22–25)

1 a Sara makes fun of someone wearing a black veil by saying, "Ninja, 10 o'clock". Why does she use the term "Ninja" and what does the time refer to?

b More seriously, what stereotypes do you use in your town or area to refer to people different from you? Do you think those people find them as funny as you do? How easy is it to find terms that are not linked to race or culture?

Monologue 5: Tahira Hussein (pages 33–36)

2 Tahira Hussein seems to have double standards. What double standards do you recognise in your own life, or those around you? How much do you sympathise with the character of Tahira, and why?

Monologue 6: Sara Jacobs (pages 36–39)

3 In many ways Eid day is like festival days in any community. Discuss some of the traditions or feelings that you identify with in this poem.

Monologue 7: Auntie Kariema (pages 39–43)

4 Discuss the problems of using such terms as "African", with its various meanings, and how difficult it can be to find neutral terms.

5 Leading on from Auntie Kariema's prejudices against Arabs, discuss dress codes, food, and holy places in various traditions and religions.

6 Refer to Auntie Kariema's description of her mother's death and how the body is prepared for burial. Every society has its own rituals and traditions surrounding death. In Western society in particular, death is often kept quite private and removed from the family. Have a general discussion about death and funerals, and also about how various societies and cultures express emotions, allowing time for personal stories if these emerge. Follow up with a journal writing exercise – this may be shared with a classmate or the educator, or kept private; it is not for assessment.

Monologue 8: Tahira Hussein (pages 43–46)

7 Following on from the description Tahira gives of the photo of the dead baby, discuss the question of civilian deaths in war. Here are some questions to provoke discussion: When are ordinary citizens (not soldiers) killed in war? How is this reported? How "allowable" are such deaths? How do terrorist attacks differ from conventional, "normal" war situations?

Monologue 9: Sara Jacobs (pages 46–47)

8 Sara talks about the truths of Islam. Do all religions have one central tenet or belief? Identify the mainstream religions in the world, for example, Buddhism, Islam, Judaism, Christianity, and so on. Try to write down one tenet or belief for each religion. Without offending anyone by saying all religions are the same, can you nevertheless find similarities between the various sayings, for example, about how we should act, or about how we should relate to God?

Extension and possible portfolio questions

English

These extension exercises and creative activities offer teachers of FAL and HL English some variety to the teaching and studying of *At Her Feet*. Some of these may be used as portfolio activities for continuous assessment purposes, as the teacher sees fit.

1 Divide into groups, where each group draws a scarf (or brings real material) to represent a different theme of the play. Learners write different aspects of the theme on their scarf or on paper and pin them to the scarf – perhaps on opposite sides of the scarf, if there are opposing views. Give each group time to tell the rest of the class about their theme-scarf. Someone could summarise them on one page, for everyone to use for revision.

2 Mecca is a holy city for Muslims. Find out more about other holy cities in Islam and other religions. Use the research to: present an oral, individually or in pairs; create a collage; write a travel diary; draw a world map identifying these sites.

3 An extension exercise to the discussion on death and the expression of emotions would be to find poems dealing with these topics. Most well-known poets have explored the theme in some way. (Possible poems and themes: war poetry; "The Lesson" by Edward Lucie Smith; Emily Dickinson's poetry.)

Dramatic Arts

These extension exercises and creative activities offer teachers of Dramatic Arts some variety to the teaching and studying of *At Her Feet*. Some of these may be used as portfolio activities for continuous assessment purposes, as the teacher sees fit.

Sound and music

In addition to the music accompanying Ayesha's slam poetry, music is used to introduce several other characters. Identify each style that would be used (not always given in the stage directions), and find examples of each. In places where there is no music, discuss why it has been omitted and whether you would, in fact, add music.

Lighting

As with the music, there are usually stage directions for very simple lighting – red, blue, harsh, or soft white. There is some symbolism here, as well as the suggestion of time of day. Learners design the lighting plan for this play.

Opening poem and Hadith

Discuss whether or not you would include the extract from "Cape Town, Jerusalem" and the Hadith in your performance of the play in some way, for example, in a written programme, or perhaps on banners around the stage. Create a programme and banners for the play in which you include these two items.

Movement

Research various religions to discover movements typical of each – for example, kneeling in certain ways, walking down a church aisle in robes, taking off one's shoes at the entrance to a mosque, spinning a prayer wheel, and so on. Practise these various movements and identify any emotions linked to them. Combine several movements into a repetitive sequence. Mime the movements of someone entering a specific place of worship, so that the audience can identify which it is (for example, mosque or church or temple or …). Are there any larger movements, such as dances, associated with some religions?

Teacher's notes

These notes have been written in order to provide support for teachers of English and Dramatic Arts who would like to use this play with their classes. They include:

- a section detailing how the play links to the National Curriculum Statement (NCS)
- a motivation for studying this play
- a discussion of the background to the play
- a description of the characters
- a synopsis of the play
- a summary of the themes
- a discussion of the theatre techniques used
- biographical information on Nadia Davids.

Teachers will find the questions on pages 52–68 useful. These include a quiz, short questions, paragraph and essay questions (all with mark allocations), more interpretive questions for discussion, activities suitable for acting out the play, and a range of activities suitable for portfolio work. The quiz and short questions are divided into those suitable for First Additional Language (FAL) learners and those suitable for Home Language (HL) learners. All the questions and activities can be used for assessment of different types. Suggested answers for all the shorter questions have been provided. There are also pointers as to what to include in the paragraph and essay questions, as well as the discussion topics.

Links to the National Curriculum Statement

This edition of *At Her Feet* is integrally linked to the curriculum in a number of different ways, as we will explain.

Links to the Critical and Developmental Outcomes

Links to the Critical Outcomes can be seen in the following ways:

- Performing and studying a play such as this will undoubtedly help learners to "work effectively with others as members of a team, group, organisation and community" (Critical Outcome 2). It will also require that learners "organise and manage themselves and

their activities responsibly and effectively" (Critical Outcome 3). Most particularly, it will develop learners' ability to "communicate effectively using visual, symbolic and/or language skills in various modes" (Critical Outcome 5).
- Working through the questions that have been included in this edition of *At Her Feet* will provide learners with the opportunity to "organise and manage themselves and their activities responsibly and effectively" (Critical Outcome 3), as marks will be awarded on the basis of how well they answer the questions. The questions also prompt learners to read, examine, evaluate, and interpret events in the play. This develops their ability to "collect, analyse, organise and critically evaluate information" (Critical Outcome 4). The questions may be used for written work or discussion, and this will hone learners' ability to "communicate effectively" (Critical Outcome 5).

In terms of the Developmental Outcomes, links can be identified as follows:
- The themes of this play – culture, tradition, religion, prejudice, basic human rights, gender bias – particularly encourage learners to work towards being "culturally and aesthetically sensitive across a range of social contexts" (Developmental Outcome 3); the most relevant and important outcome for literature. They also prompt learners to think about how they can "participate as responsible citizens in the life of local, national and global communities" (Developmental Outcome 2).
- Some learners might take the opportunity to explore a facet of theatre as a career, for example, acting, dancing, sound and lighting, special effects, directing, producing, or writing. By studying this play learners could be helped to "explore education and career opportunities" (Developmental Outcome 4).

Links to principles of the National Curriculum Statement

We believe that this play will give learners the opportunity to reflect on and develop their understanding of certain principles of the NCS, in particular, principle 1: "social transformation" and principle 7: "human rights, inclusivity, environmental and social justice".

Principle 1 states that "all South Africans have to be educationally affirmed through the recognition of their potential". This play with its focus on women's "voices" will powerfully recognise and affirm many female learners.

An important theme in *At Her Feet* is that of gender and race identities and how complex these are. As learners explore this theme they will be dealing with issues of inclusivity and social justice, as well as human rights, and developing a good understanding of them (principal 7).

Fulfilling the requirements for assessment in literature

The Subject Assessment Guidelines for Languages outline the following requirements for Grades 10–12:

Language	Paper	Contents and marks
Home Language	Paper 2 (literature) 80 marks	Poetry (30 marks) + novel (25 marks) + drama (25 marks)
First Additional Language	Paper 2 (literature) 70 marks	Any TWO of these genres: novel (35 marks)/ drama (35 marks)/short stories (35 marks)/ poetry (35 marks)

Learning Outcomes for activities and assessment

We spoke to many teachers in different parts of South Africa to find out what they wanted in drama for high school. They told us that they wanted plays that were:

- fresh, with themes that their learners could identify with
- short or one-act
- meaty enough to discuss in class and set essays and questions on
- South African.

They also told us that they wanted both short and long questions on the plays, with mark allocations where appropriate.

We believe we have met all of these needs, including the request for activities. These follow the play, encouraging learners to engage with the text in a variety of ways. The activities can be assessed using various methods, including peer, group, pair, teacher, portfolio and self assessment, and will help learners fulfil the Learning Outcomes for Language, particularly aspects of Learning Outcome 2: Reading and viewing, as noted here.

Learning Outcomes for Language

Home Language

Grade 10 *LO2 AS4: Literary texts (drama and film study)*

- Explain the link between dialogue and action, and the characters and the theme.
- Explain plot, subplot, character portrayal, conflict, and dramatic purpose.
- Identify dramatic structure and interpret stage directions.

Grade 11 *LO2 AS4: Literary texts (drama and film study)*

- Analyse dialogue and action, and their relation to character and theme.
- Evaluate plot, subplot, character portrayal, conflict, dramatic purpose, and dramatic irony.
- Interpret and explain dramatic structure and stage directions.

Grade 12 *LO2 AS4: Literary texts (drama and film study)*

- Analyse dialogue and action, and their relation to character and theme.
- Evaluate plot, subplot, character portrayal, conflict, dramatic purpose, and dramatic irony.
- Interpret, explain and evaluate dramatic structure and stage directions.

First Additional Language

Grade 10 *LO2 AS4: Explore key features of texts and explain how they contribute to meaning – literary texts (drama and film study)*

- Recognise how dialogue and action are related to character and theme.
- Describe plot, subplot, character portrayal, conflict, and dramatic purpose.
- Recognise the uses of dramatic structure and stage directions.

Grade 11 *LO2 AS4: Explore key features of texts and explain how they contribute to meaning – literary texts (drama and film study)*

- Recognise how dialogue and action are related to character and theme.
- Explain plot, subplot, character portrayal, conflict, dramatic purpose, and dramatic irony.
- Explain dramatic structure and stage directions.

Grade 12 *LO2 AS4: Explore key features of texts and explain how they contribute to meaning – literary texts (drama and film study)*

- Recognise how dialogue and action are related to character and theme.
- Explain and interpret plot, subplot, character portrayal, conflict, dramatic purpose, and dramatic irony.
- Explain and interpret dramatic structure and stage directions.

Learning Outcomes for Dramatic Arts

LO1: Apply Personal Resources and *LO2: Create, Make and Present*
Made up of eleven realistic, intimate monologues by six different women characters, the play provides ample scope for applying personal resources and presenting dramatic performances.

LO3: Understand and Analyse
With themes addressing race and gender issues, this play provides an excellent example of how the Dramatic Arts can both affirm and challenge values, societies, cultures, and identities within a context that is uniquely South African yet universally applicable. There is also wide scope for independent research.

LO4: Reflect and Evaluate
The play provides learners with the opportunity to "respond to others' drama with empathy and sensitivity in order to address prejudice, stereotyping and bigotry", as it contains examples of these issues on various levels.

Note: Learning Outcomes and other curriculum material have been taken from the National Curriculum Statement and other Department of Education documents. Please consult the full documents for more information. Also see <http://www.education.gov.za/Curriculum/LPGs2007/LPG%20LANGUAGES.pdf>

A motivation for studying this play

In her insightful, comprehensive foreword, Gabeba Baderoon offers many compelling reasons to read and see this play – reasons that readily translate to studying it in a classroom context.

First of all, it is South African and contemporary in its references and realistic dialogue, yet it also makes use of poetic language, allusions, and memories. Funny, clever and energetic, it is not awkwardly serious or trying to teach a moral lesson, yet it addresses many important moral issues in its themes. The reader is drawn in by the structure of the play, as the characters often address the audience directly in their monologues. The structure is simple but not repetitive, the characters ordinary but not predictable. While there is no climax to the action of the play – Azra speaks of her death almost in the opening lines – the final scene with Azra's mother is unexpected and deeply moving.

At Her Feet is a play presented by Muslim women, but the issues they present confront everyone – as the playwright says on page 11, "I believe I would have written about these things through different stories had I been born into a different set of circumstances – I have simply used the prism I have been given." The play is challenging yet sensitive, and the playwright comments that, "it is not [her] aim to be disrespectful" (page 14) – there are no obvious barriers or social taboos in the text.

Finally, this is a play that can easily be read aloud in class, presented in a play-reading, or staged with its minimal props and costume requirements.

Background to the play

Cape Town and its communities

The play is set in Cape Town, in the opening decade of the twenty-first century. The place has its own unique blend of cultures and races, with the play focusing specifically on the Muslim community of Cape Town. The characters are all representative of this sometimes divided community: people who are proud of their Malay heritage; those of Indian origin; those who are more "Arab" in appearance and speech; and those who don't fit into any of these groups. Auntie Kariema uses terms to talk about Islam that are of Malaysian origin, and is scornful of those who have adopted Arabic terms. She also mixes her languages, often slipping into Afrikaans, the language traditionally associated with the Cape coloured community. She and others also reflect the racism inherent in their community (but not exclusive to it), looking down on those with "*kroes*" or curly hair as having black African ancestry and so being somehow inferior.

There are various references to Cape Town shopping centres, shops and designers, but these are easily understood in context and may be substituted in discussion with similar local names.

The character of Azra is Jordanian, but there is little reference to the actual place. The desert setting is described by the character, but it is otherwise more a personal space than a realistic one.

Honour killings

In some Muslim communities, a woman who has broken the very strict laws governing male-female relationships is seen as having dishonoured her whole family. The men of the family are expected to remove the dishonour, to "cleanse their name", by killing the woman, who may be a sister, wife, or mother to them. The woman may be stoned to death as described in this play, or killed some other way. According to Jordanian law, a woman who is suspected of adultery or an illegal act may be killed by her husband or close male relatives, and the men will only receive a light sentence or none at all for the action.

In around 2001, Muslim shari'ah law was introduced in several states in Nigeria and several cases of women being sentenced to death made world news and were widely debated. One in particular was that of Amina Lawal, a thirty-one-year-old pregnant woman from Katsina State, who was found guilty of adultery under shari'ah law in 2002 and was sentenced to death by stoning. The father of her child was not prosecuted for lack of evidence. With the help of two women's rights groups in Nigeria, Amina appealed against the verdict and, more than a year later, her conviction was overturned by a panel of judges.

In some communities, just speaking to a man without a male relative or an older woman present may be seen as bringing dishonour; in others, it might be the act of marrying a man not chosen by the woman's family. As we see in this play, members of the Muslim community, as in many religious and other communities, do not always agree on every aspect of their beliefs.

September 11, 2001

This day is also referred to as nine eleven (9/11). On this date, nineteen terrorists hijacked four American passenger planes. Two planes were flown into the Twin Towers of the World Trade Centre in New York City, a third crashed into the Pentagon (headquarters of the USA Department of Defence), and the fourth crashed after passengers and crew tried to regain control of the plane. No one on board any of the planes survived, and the final number of people killed in the attacks was close to three thousand. The victims came from over ninety countries.

After this attack, many countries strengthened their laws against terrorism and the US declared a "War on Terrorism", particularly focusing on al-Qaeda, the group responsible for the attacks. This group's motivation was partly political, but also religious: an Islamist group, they targeted America for being anti-Islam. As a result of this association between terrorism and Islam, there was a worldwide response against Muslim and even Middle-Eastern-looking people. While most Muslims condemned the attacks, some people harassed and attacked those seen to be of Muslim faith, often mistakenly, as in the case of Sikhs who wear turbans but are in fact not Muslim. In the play, Tahira's wedding on 1 September is closely followed by the 9/11 attacks. As a Muslim, she wears a headscarf to work, leading to her boss complaining that customers are scared of buying tickets from her because of the association between Muslims and terrorism.

Characters in the play

This section takes the character list as its basis, adding quotes from the text together with commentary to provide a character sketch of each woman. As the play develops, we gain information from the stage directions and from the way each character comments on other characters, building up a picture of each woman.

Azra al Jamal

A young Jordanian Muslim woman, stoned to death in an "honour" killing. She gives us a lyrical, moving account of her own death – the punishment of silence, for daring to speak to a man who is not related to her.

Sara Jacobs

The play's storyteller is a South African Muslim woman in her twenties, who lives in Cape Town. She is described as "thoughtful and reflective, given to bursts of energetic impersonation". The killing of Azra disturbs her and makes her question how her faith is lived out in practice, and these questions are woven through the play in conversations with her friends and relatives.

"I wonder if I don't wear one [a scarf] simply because I don't like what it says./Or maybe it's because I don't want you looking at me, the way you look at them."

Auntie Kariema

Sara's aunt (on her mother's side) is a middle-aged Muslim woman who lives in Cape Town and identifies herself as "Malay". From the outset she is intolerant of many things, such as Western music and people of Indian descent – even though they may be Muslim. Sara's father's family is Indian or "*charra*". Auntie Kariema works hard to please her family with her cooking, and by the end of the play she is a character with whom we have some sympathy, despite her intolerances.

Ayesha

Sara's friend, Ayesha, is a young Muslim feminist slam-poetess who lives in Cape Town. She is passionate about her political beliefs, although a little vague about the details. She too has her prejudices, feeling that Tahira and her friends who look "more Muslim than I do" are superficial and too consumerist. She does genuinely try to adhere to the spiritual purpose of the Ramadan fast – the only character who seems to do so.

Tahira Hussein

Sara's cousin is Tahira, a newly-married Indian-Muslim woman who works for a travel agency in Cape Town. "She is a little superficial and catty, but is fundamentally a good person." She has to deal with various forms of racism in the course of her work. Like Kariema and Ayesha, she has her prejudices – she comments that Ayesha "doesn't really belong ...", yet also says that "we [Muslim people] need to stand together". Like many women, she likes to spoil her husband, and she worries about the future for her unborn child.

Azra's mother

The Jordanian girl's mother. Her dance-like movements echo her daughter's dance at the start of the play. She speaks as a Muslim woman, articulating the fears and silences of many. She also speaks as a mother, promising not to forget her daughter.

A synopsis of the play

The play is not divided into scenes, but consists rather of a series of monologues or reflections that become conversations with the audience.

Poem and Hadith

The lines from the poem, "Cape Town, Jerusalem" speak of the poet's search for words to explain (or "house") the Muslim culture ("my tribe") – and the inadequacy of words to do so.

The Hadith (sayings of the Prophet Mohamed) is echoed in the words of Azra's mother in the final monologue. It suggests a reverence for motherhood, an ideal image of women, sharply contrasted with the death of the Jordanian girl.

Monologue 1: Azra al Jamal

"My name is Azra al Jamal and I have just been killed."

Azra graphically yet lyrically describes her own stoning, how she lies exposed for all to see, no longer "pure and unsoiled". She mentions "this cloth" and how speaking through it "is not allowed". She asks if "you" (the audience) remember her name.

Monologue 2: Sara Jacobs

Sara's poem about the scarf worn by Muslim women begins to explore the theme of being silent behind the veil, ("the geometry of silence"). She describes her reaction to viewing a documentary on the stoning, wondering about the connection between her and other Muslim women, between her and this woman, "my sister". She describes how she has grown up watching women choose and wear scarves, how it is part of her too, although she wears it differently because "I don't want you looking at me, the way you look at them".

Monologue 3: Auntie Kariema

In this monologue Auntie Kariema responds to Sara's news about the death of the Jordanian woman, talking to Sara as if she were sitting in her kitchen. She says that if the girl broke the rules she must be punished and then goes on to blame the influence of Western culture, and music in particular. She makes sweeping generalisations and unblinkingly justifies her own TV-watching habits, while condemning others for even listening to a particular style of music. She goes on to show her bias against people of Indian origin, even though they may also be Muslims and are related to her by marriage. She repeats that disobedience deserves punishment.

Monologue 4: Ayesha

Ayesha outlines her politics, wearing iconic symbols with passion but having a rather vague understanding of the theory behind them. Like Auntie Kariema, she easily justifies her own motives while condemning others. Giving a comic impersonation of the snobbish, fashionable Shamiela, Ayesha too describes prejudices within the Muslim community, assumptions people make based on looks and style of dress. She mentions that she takes the Ramadan fast seriously, and covers her head when leaving the house. She goes on to relate how she was dating Nazeem, Sara's cousin and Auntie Kariema's son. She discovered he was avoiding taking her home because he knew his mother would see her "*kroes*" hair and assume she was not Muslim. Hearing this information was like having "emotional rocks thrown" at her. She retaliated by buying a wig of straight hair so that he could take her home as promised – but omitted to tell him the wig was blonde! After the visit she broke up with him, refusing a lift with the defiantly funny line: "*... ek en my hare gaan huis toe.*"

Monologue 5: Tahira Hussein

Tahira's monologue introduces us to some of the stereotypes that non-Muslims have of Muslims. She fends off lewd suggestions and, much more seriously, must stop wearing her scarf at work or lose her job (see September 11 background on pages 75–76). As well as disapproving of Ayesha, she comments that Ayesha doesn't really belong, a reference again to her looks as well as to her lifestyle. Like Kariema and Ayesha, Tahira is gentle on herself while condemning the same faults in others – a very human failing that draws sympathy from the audience.

Monologue 6: Sara Jacobs

Sara describes and discusses the Ramadan fast (a month during which, from sunrise to sunset, Muslims do not eat), and how it defines the community and draws it together. She comments on how Eid day (the end of the month of Ramadan) is "so different if you are a boy"; describes the "Eid fashion show"; and puts on a fez (man's hat) for a poem describing the prayers, family visits, and parade of clothes and accessories that make up Eid day. The poem explores the various contradictions of the day: holy day and high fashion; visiting elderly relatives and hanging out with other teenagers; girls in mini-skirts but still wearing scarves.

Monologue 7: Auntie Kariema

We find Kariema facing the washing up at the end of Eid day. She comments on Sara's liberalism and how she calls herself an African, a term Auntie Kariema clearly disapproves of. She has some harsh things to say about Arabs and their "ownership" of Islam. She is staunchly Malay, and makes annoying and upsetting remarks about the "*charras*". She refers again to the death of the Jordanian girl. Her first response is, "Well you know what? Life is unfair" but then finds common ground when she relates the story of her mother. She tells of learning to cook and then describes her mother's early death and how she "needed to bury (her) mother", but was not allowed, by Muslim custom, to walk in the funeral procession. "So this girl, this Arab girl. I suppose I can understand her … I wanted to walk [in my mother's funeral procession], she wanted to talk [to a man who was not family]."

Monologue 8: Tahira Hussein

Tahira tells how she has left her job, of the baby shower her friends give her, her hidden dislike of her mother-in-law who openly checks on her daughter-in-law's housekeeping. She gives an account of seeing a picture of a dead baby in the newspaper, her reply to someone's comment on it, and her worries about bringing a baby into the world.

Monologue 9: Sara Jacobs

Sara describes bored afternoons in the Madressa as a child. From this description she explores her understanding of the Arabic language and Islam and its place in her life, ending with a direct challenge to the wearing of a scarf: "I don't believe that any of that [the truths of Islam] depends on making sure I wear this [the scarf]."

Monologue 10: Ayesha

Ayesha's poem "Ms Islam" is a slam poem, a performance piece set to music as described in the stage directions. She touches on the divisions that gender brings, unbending laws, the sisterhood of Islam, her own questions, ways to freedom. Then the tone is more urgent as the music changes and she mentions the struggles of Muslim women – sisters – in various countries and ending in Cape Town, concluding with these challenging questions: "where my roots?/And where are my sisters?"

Monologue 11: Azra's mother

Azra's mother speaks to her dead daughter as she cradles her head in her lap. She speaks of her birth, of how a girl is a prisoner of her own body, wrapped and hidden. She takes possession of her daughter, sure that she is in Paradise, assuring her that "I will not forget".

A summary of the themes

In her notes (pages 9–11) the playwright identifies the issues that act as themes within the play when she writes, "The issues that I wanted to trace around culture, tradition, religion, prejudice, inalienable rights, gender bias, and discrimination ... ". Part of what she explores is the way in which all these things are bound together, and how they influence us to varying degrees. It is at times, therefore, quite difficult to simplify the themes and separate them – they are all threads in the veil, patterns on the scarf.

In the first monologue we are introduced to the veil, "this cloth" and the silence it imposes on women. Azra suffers the worst possible consequence of breaking this silence. So Sara in her first scene speaks of the "geometry of silence", beginning to voice the doubts that other Muslim women may not voice. In the interview (pages 12–17), Nadia asks, "Why are Muslim women not given the space to air their doubts and beliefs?" By the end of the play many women have spoken through the six characters, and while Azra's mother says there are "no words" for her daughter, she promises (along with those listening in the audience) to remember.

Inextricably linked to the veil or scarf is the question of who imposes its use: do women wear it by choice, or do they wear it because it is enforced by a rigid – at times violent – patriarchal (male-dominated) society? Sara's first poem uses metaphors to explore this theme: the "silken noose", "heads misty-chained". She cannot ignore these issues that are central to Muslim women: "The scarf is part of me, whether I accept or reject it."

The theme of sisterhood, of a unity between women who share a common faith, indeed between women no matter what their faith, emerges at the outset. The concept is tested and explored in the various women's relationships that form the play.

With the character of Auntie Kariema, the themes of race and religion emerge, combining questions about South African Muslim identity, and further touching on many of the issues named by the playwright. When Ayesha speaks, she voices the feelings of one of those against whom Auntie Kariema is prejudiced. Ayesha speaks of the prejudice as "emotional rocks thrown" at her – and the rocks are thrown by members of her own Muslim community. They cannot kill her, as they do Azra, but the symbolic connection is clear.

The themes of race and religion continue in Tahira's monologues – both the subtle forms of prejudice within the Muslim culture, and the more obvious prejudices of those who are of a different race and religion. Basic human rights and discrimination are also at issue here.

Theatre techniques

The contemporary nature of the play is discussed in the synopsis of the play, while the section on themes addresses issues of culture and universality.

Realism

The play is a series of realistic monologues – conversations with other characters or the audience, and also internal reflection. The style relies on building a relationship between each character and the audience, rather than between characters on stage.

Poetry

Some monologues are more lyrical than others, while several contain poetry in various styles – some simply spoken, some spoken to music. This offers a different challenge to that of the realistic monologue style.

Sound and music

In addition to the music accompanying Ayesha's slam poetry, music introduces several characters. Learners would need to identify each style (not always given in the stage directions) and find examples of each. In places where there is no music, they could discuss why it has been omitted and whether they would in fact add music.

Lighting

As with the music, there are usually stage directions to very simple lighting – red, blue, harsh, or soft white. There is some symbolism here, as well as the suggestion of time of day. Designing the lighting plan would be simple yet challenging enough for Grade 10 learners.

Costumes and props

These are realistic yet simple. There are one or two different tops and/or scarves for each character, with hooks or a rail for these; a chair and stool, and a table; a box of scarves. Colours, styles, and the practical issues of changing can all be discussed and attempted.

Symbols

These are addressed in notes on the themes and the plot, and through various questions. There is strong visual symbolism in the central motif of the scarf.

Staging

This play presents few constraints in terms of budget, being simple to stage in terms of lighting, props, and costumes. One could consider allocating each character to a different actress for a school production – learners could be involved in working out the changes to script and action that this might necessitate.

Biographical information on the playwright

Nadia Davids has been "writing and making theatre" from childhood. Her first production was *Khumbula*, which she staged in 1995 at the Grahamstown Festival during her Grade 12 year. Since then she has written and produced *Cissie*, a play about the District Six activist, Cissie Gool. The play was nominated for three Fleur de Cap awards, including "Best New South African Play" and won Best Supporting Actress. Nadia's other writings range from *The littlest warrior*, a play based on the traditional African narrative style called *instomi* and published by Oxford University Press in 2007 in a volume called *South African Plays for TV, Radio and Stage*, and published short stories, such as "The healer", "Safe home", and "The visit". In the Southern African PEN Literary Awards adjudicated by JM Coetzee, "Safe home" was a finalist in 2007 and "The visit" was placed third in 2009.

In 2008, Nadia was awarded a PhD in Drama from the University of Cape Town. Her thesis topic was "Inherited Memories, Performing the Archive; an exploration of performances of loss, memory and mourning of District Six, South Africa".

Born and educated in South Africa, this gifted writer now divides her time between Cape Town, New York, and London. In 2008 she was one of ten playwrights worldwide to be invited to participate in the two-year Playwrights' Lab at The Women's Project Theatre in New York. Prior to that, her work in the United States included invitations to the University of California, Berkeley, and to New York University as a visiting scholar and instructor for Special Programs, South Africa. Nadia takes up a full-time teaching post in the Queen Mary's College, University of London's Drama Department in 2009.

Nadia Davids has been called "one of South Africa's most talented and up-and-coming writers" (*UK Guardian*, 2007) and her work has been described as giving "voice to the voiceless" (*Cape Times*, 2003). We eagerly anticipate her next play.

Suggested answers

Pre-reading activities (pages 52–53)

5 Ways in which you can check your facts: ask Muslim learners in the class or school; consult the local Muslim mosque or school; use books and the Internet.

6 How these terms are related to one another:
Prejudice is a preconceived opinion; bias is a synonym for prejudice (usually more favourable than prejudice); discrimination is selection for unfavourable treatment, based on race or other difference. In other words, discrimination is a result of prejudice.

Quiz (pages 53–54)

1 B (they want to restore their honour) ✓ (1)
2 D (an Indian) ✓ (1)
3 B (niece) ✓ (1)
4 A (husband) ✓ (1)
5 C (she is pregnant) ✓ (1)
6 B (Che Guevara) ✓ (1)
7 Cape Town (note: Azra and her mother are from the country of Jordan) ✓ (1)
8 Islam ✓ (1)
9 Afrikaans; ✓Arabic; ✓Malay ✓ (3)
10 Jordan ✓ (1)
11 Ayesha's hair is very curly ("*kroes*") ✓and he says his mother might think she is African and not Muslim. ✓ (2)
12 People thought, wrongly, ✓ that they were Muslim. ✓ (Learners could discuss generalisations and stereotypes following this question.) (2)
13 Gender bias. ✓ The play deals mostly with the difficulties, prejudices, and lack of choice facing Muslim women. ✓ (2)
14 Positive. ✓ "You are in the arms of the Most Merciful, and at the feet of the Infinitely Compassionate." ✓ OR "I will not forget." ✓ (2)

Short questions

Monologue 1: Azra Al Jamal

First Additional Language (pages 54–55)

1 italics vs normal font; ✓ third person vs first person narration ✓ (2)
2 music; ✓ lighting; ✓ actor's movements; ✓ costume/clothing ✓ (4)
3 The *hijab* would cover hair, ears, and neck completely, ✓ while the

burkha over this covers a woman from head to toe, covering the face also. ✓ (Ask Art or Consumer Studies learners to draw these garments.) (2)

Home Language (page 55)

1 The plan should show correct interpretation of stage right and left, space open in centre, and so on. Here is one possible arrangement. (6)

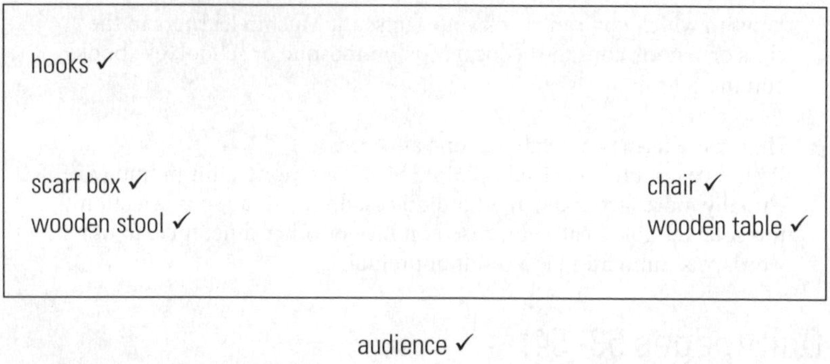

2 This is a guide: The character is in a spotlight (stage directions). ✓ She refers to midday heat, so there could be white or yellow light; ✓ but she also refers to seeing only night, so the light might dim at that point or become less yellow. ✓ (3)

3 the veil; ✓ patriarchy ✓ (2)

4 This is a guide: *Diction*: Her mouth bleeds "softly", an unexpected word here; ✓✓ *Figurative language*: she is "curled up in an awkward zero, … circling (her) own end"; the shape of her body is also a metaphor for death, for nothing, for zero; ✓✓ OR "light is pouring in over secrets": this is both literal (she is outside, punished for all to see) and figurative (she cannot hide her wrongdoing). ✓✓ OR "heard [the stars] moan anxiously down at me" could be part of her death experience as she can't literally hear them and stars are traditionally used as a metaphor for fate in literature; ✓✓ *Repetition*: "my name", a desperate plea to be remembered/not forgotten. ✓✓ (two good points = 4)

Monologue 2: Sara Jacobs

First Additional Language (page 55)

1 The scarf is folded into a triangle ✓ and Egyptian pyramids are triangular in shape; ✓ Pythagoras was a mathematician who wrote theorems to explain triangles. ✓ (3)

2 a Scarves are worn to keep hair hidden ✓ as it is supposedly too tempting for men to see. ✓ (2)

b veils; ✓ patriarchy ✓ (2)

3 thoughtful/reflective/non-judgemental ✓✓

(any two appropriate adjectives = 2)

Home Language (pages 55–56)

1 a The scarf is worn to hide hair, which is regarded as seductive.✓ (1)
  b No. ✓ Reference to dead tendrils ✓ is somewhat scathing – it undermines ✓ the reason, even as it presents it. (3)
2 a *Noose*: hangman's noose is linked to death; ✓ *chained*: imprisoned ✓ in some way. (2)
  b These words refer to the patriarchal society ✓ that wants to keep women in check, temptation under wraps, seductive voices silenced. ✓ The rule is for the benefit of men, not women. ✓ (3)
3 "You know how good Arabs are at throwing rocks." ✓ (1)

Monologue 3: Auntie Kariema

First Additional Language (page 56)

1 She is talking to Sara ✓ about the killing of the Jordanian girl. ✓ (2)
2 "Ag, no man!"/"Ag" ✓ (1)
3 They are Sara's father's family, ✓ while Auntie Kariema is related to Sara's mother. ✓ (2)
4 She dislikes the bare tummies shown by a sari, and dancing; ✓ their making money; ✓ their wearing lots of gold – it's flashy, showing off.✓ (two points = 2)
5 She shows prejudice and bias within culture. ✓ She provides a character who is a typical wife and mother, ✓and happily so. ✓ (3)

Home Language (page 56)

1 She is constantly moving, chopping, etc. ✓ She asks many questions ✓ – her speech is thus "active", interactive, as she talks with Sara. (2)
2 a She says Western music and singers are a bad influence, ✓ yet she herself listens to and watches them. ✓ (2)
  b She justifies this by saying her husband has paid ✓ for satellite, so she must watch it. ✓ (2)
3 The playwright describes her as "bigoted" – unwilling to accept opinions that differ from her own. ✓ Auntie Kariema voices several opinions through which the playwright explores prejudice within ✓ the Muslim culture and religion, for example, her anti-Indian remarks, ✓ and her judgement ✓ of the Jordanian girl. (4)

Monologue 4: Ayesha

First Additional Language (page 57)

1 The audience can identify with how she talks ✓ in a very ordinary, South African way, ✓ like any teenager or young adult might, even though they might not agree with her politics. (2)

2

Tahira and Shamiela	Ayesha	Theme
They think Ayesha: • *does not look Muslim* • is not very religious ✓ • does not have much dress sense ✓	*She thinks they:* • *are snobbish about their Malay ancestry* • are superficial in their religion ✓ • spend too much time and money on clothes ✓	• *Prejudices about culture* • Prejudices about religion ✓ • Consumerism – clash of culture and religion ✓

(6)

Home Language (page 57)

1 They obviously spend a lot of time and money ✓ on what they wear, trying to be fashionable and "in". ✓ Through Ayesha, the playwright is commenting on the consumerism ✓ that is at odds with Islamic faith. ✓ (See also Sara's "Eid Day" poem, Monologue 6.) (4)

2 a Azra dies for her wrong relationship, ✓ while Ayesha suffers emotional hurt ✓ at prejudice within a relationship. (2)

b Azra feels powerless ✓ to act against her cultural restrictions. ✓ Ayesha, on the other hand, can think of how to react ("my mind reeled with solutions") ✓ and has some power ✓ over the situation. (4)

Monologue 5: Tahira Hussein

First Additional Language (page 58)

1 She criticises Ayesha for drinking ✓ yet admits that many others do it and that she herself smokes. ✓ OR She upholds certain morals ✓ herself, yet says Ayesha must "get off her moral high horse". ✓ OR She says Muslims must stand together, ✓ not criticise each other, yet she herself criticises Ayesha. ✓ (2)

2 "you people" is a subtly racist ✓✓ generalisation. (2)

3 Yes, he is justified. ✓ He is losing business ✓ because customers react negatively ✓ to Tahira's headscarf.

No, he is not justified. ✓ He should help change ✓ the stereotype, not reinforce ✓ it by asking her to change. OR His supposed liberal views (he is a DP supporter) should be inclusive, ✓ allowing her freedom of religious expression. ✓

Not sure. ✓ Offer one argument on either side of the argument. ✓✓ (3)

Home Language (page 58)

1 She criticises Ayesha for drinking, yet admits many others do it and that she herself smokes. ✓ OR She upholds certain morals herself, yet says Ayesha must "get off her moral high horse". ✓ OR She says Muslims must stand together, not criticise each other, yet she herself criticises Ayesha. ✓

Learners should then comment on similar examples they see around them, such as friends who demand loyalty yet are not loyal themselves. ✓ (2)

2 The theme is racism ✓ as the phrase "you people" is a subtly racist ✓ generalisation. (2)

3 a Mr Talbot implies that he is losing business ✓ because customers react negatively ✓ to Tahira's headscarf. (2)

b You might argue that he should help change ✓ the stereotype, not reinforce ✓ it by asking her to change. OR His supposed liberal (DP) views should be inclusive, ✓allowing her freedom of religious expression. ✓ (2)

Monologue 6: Sara Jacobs

First Additional Language (page 58)

1 Only the Muslims are up so early, ✓ needing to switch lights on as they eat ✓ before sunrise during Ramadan. (2)

2 There is a positive sense of community and sharing, ✓ even though the society is still divided. However, while boys have freedom and friendship, girls stay at home – this inequality is a negative aspect. ✓ (2)

3 morning prayers at the mosque; ✓ afternoon family visits; ✓ evening parade at the malls ✓ (3)

Home Language (page 59)

1 *Use of alliteration*: "*f*ast *f*all in *f*ractured". ✓ *Senses*: the air thick and velvety" (touch), "spiced beef … and … tea" (taste). ✓ *Play on words*: "half-muted darkness" (muted can mean the sounds are muffled; muted can also mean subdued or not bright in colour). ✓ (any two examples) These examples show Sara to be a poetic and thoughtful person. ✓ (3)

2 Ayesha mentions focusing on the poor ✓ in the fast period, whereas the Eid parade is lavish and expensive ✓ – seeming at odds with the goal of the whole month. There is also an underlying conflict ✓ here, between Islam with its fasting and holding back, and Western consumerist culture. (3)

3 pictures of the Ka'aba; ✓ a wife who "lives softly silently" reminding us that women are not allowed to voice issues ✓ (Note that the latter is not exclusive to the Muslim community.) (2)

Monologue 7: Auntie Kariema

First Additional Language (page 59)

1 She likes to cook for her family. ✓ She boasts ✓ about her cooking. She can't understand ✓ her child's new tastes. (3)

2 She labels all "whiteys" ✓ as "liberal". ✓ (2)

3 She is racist when it comes to black or African people. ✓ (1)

4 They both did something they were not allowed to do. ✓ In remembering how badly she needed to do what she tried to do, ✓ Auntie Kariema

is able to understand how badly Azra needed to do what she did – she understands her motives. ✓ "I wanted to walk [in the funeral procession], she wanted to talk [on her own, to a man not related to her]." ✓ (4)

Home Language (pages 59–60)

1 She says they "act like they own Islam" ✓ (because the holy city of Mecca is in Saudi Arabia). They seem to have double standards, ✓ the women dress one way outdoors and another way indoors. Malaysians have given a halaal food (beef) a haraam flavour ✓ (bacon) when Muslims may not eat pork. (Note: it is more important to identify the prejudice, than remember its exact details.) (3)

2 a They both did something they were not allowed to do. ✓ (1)

b Auntie Kariema wanted to follow the men and bury her mother. ✓ Azra wanted to talk on her own to a man not related to her. ✓ (2)

c The theme of gender bias ✓ is explored here. Implicit in this statement are these questions: Why should men be allowed to attend a funeral, and women not? ✓ Why may a man approach a woman and speak to her, but not vice versa? ✓ (3)

3 Once more, Auntie Kariema is doing something she probably judges in others, but allows for herself. ✓ (Smoking is frowned on by Islam, but widely practised.) Here, however, her smoking highlights her deep emotion, ✓ an emotion that allows her to identify ✓ with Azra. (3)

Monologue 8: Tahira Hussein

First Additional Language (page 60)

1 a She is pregnant. ✓ (1)

b *Positive consequence*: She now has time to herself. ✓ OR She is less stressed. ✓

Negative consequence: She does get lonely. ✓ OR They can't buy their own home. ✓ (2)

2 She doesn't get on well with her. ✓ Her mother-in-law seems to interfere, rather than help. ✓ (2)

3 a She sees a picture of a baby with blood on its head. ✓ It still has its dummy in its mouth. ✓ (2)

b She will soon have a baby of her own. ✓ OR The baby has been killed. ✓ OR The man in the queue seems to think the baby deserved to die. ✓ (1)

Home Language (page 60)

1 a She thinks she knows better about what her son wants or likes. ✓ OR She is interfering. ✓ (1)

b Most people recognise ✓ the mother-in-law stereotype and will laugh at her interfering ✓ but this also makes us sympathetic towards Tahira – no one likes to be told ✓ how to cook or do things, especially in the close relationship of marriage. (3)

2 It might have been killed in an air raid/bombing ✓ by American soldiers ✓ acting against suspected terrorists. ✓ (3)

Monologue 9: Sara Jacobs

First Additional Language (page 61)

1 No.✓ "would stir something" ✓ (2)

2 She does not believe that there is a vital connection – the truth will stand with or without the scarf. ✓✓ (2)

Home Language (page 61)

1 Most, if not all, religions are sometimes boring. ✓ Children the world over struggle to be self-disciplined, and to sit still and learn. ✓ Anyone can identify with the naughty friend. ✓ People will easily identify with reciting something they don't fully understand. ✓

(any two points = 2)

2 She doesn't necessarily question the truth itself, but the way in which it is practised, ✓ saying that she doesn't believe that wearing a scarf ✓ is crucial to maintaining ✓ the central truth of her faith. (3)

Monologue 10: Ayesha

First Additional Language (page 61)

1 The poem focuses most obviously on gender bias, ✓ which contains elements of these other themes in the play: culture, tradition and religion, indisputable human rights, and discrimination. There are also references to women across cultures and times, ✓and to human rights issues other than gender bias. ✓ (3)

2 "Paradise lies at the feet of mothers" – Hadith ✓ (see page 20) (1)

Home Language (page 62)

1 *Repetition*: "To my sisters" is repeated, giving the poem structure and reinforcing the idea of a sisterhood. ✓✓ OR Several words are repeated, emphasising the idea or emotion dealt with. ✓✓ OR Several phrases are either repeated or subtly altered in the repetition, again to emphasise a point or make a contrast. ✓✓

Play on words: "routes" and "roots" – this makes an instant connection between the ideas, without needing a wordy explanation. ✓✓

Rhyme: For example, "earth", "worth" (stanza 1); "ending", 'bending" (stanza 2); "whispers", "sisters" and "wife", "life" (stanza 3); "head", "thread", "dread" (stanza 4)– these rhyming words serve to link these ideas. ✓✓

Rhythm: to some extent this is provided by the background music but the repetition also forms a certain rhythm.✓✓

(2 marks per device and effect = 4)

2 *The divisions that gender brings*: "who would have thought that physical bodies would/render them [souls] apart"; ✓ *unbending laws*: "there is no bending"; ✓ *the sisterhood of Islam*: "my global Ummah sisters"; ✓ *her own questions*: "... can't make sense of the voices"; ✓ *ways to freedom*: "journeys ... routes to freedom" ✓ (5)

3 Sara challenges the wearing of headscarves. ✓✓ Ayesha broadens this to address deeper gender divisions, and other violations of human rights. ✓✓ (4)

Monologue 11: Azra's mother

First Additional Language (page 62)

1 daughter: blue light; dance movements ✓✓
mother: red light; dance movements ✓✓ (4)

2 a She describes Paradise, ✓speaking as a mother. (1)
b It is positive/reassuring because the mother expresses the certainty that her daughter's suffering has ended as she is now "in the arms of the Most Merciful, and at the feet of the Infinitely Compassionate." ✓✓ OR It is positive/reassuring because her daughter will live on in her memory – "I will not forget". ✓✓ (2)

Home Language (page 62)

1 Like her daughter, Azra's mother dances. ✓ Here, though, the lighting is red, whereas it is blue in Azra's scene. ✓ (2)

2 It provides a focus and possibly action for the actress. ✓ It is intensely moving, as the mother is speaking to her daughter, not just in her thoughts, but to her dead body. ✓ (2)

3 She will remember her daughter. ✓She is able to embrace her. ✓She voices her certainty that her daughter is in Paradise or heaven. ✓ (3)

Paragraph questions (pages 63–64)

Paragraph questions can be marked out of 10–15 marks, and the answers are usually around 80–150 words long. Check the latest Subject Assessment Guidelines (SAG) for exam requirements.

These answers are merely guidelines:

1 Each character reflects on Azra's death in some way either directly, like Sara and Auntie Kariema, or indirectly, like Ayesha and Tahira. Learners should relate each character's reflections proportionally. See the interview with Nadia where she speaks of how the play is "book-ended by two symbolic … slices" (page 14), i.e. Azra's and her mother's scenes, while the rest of the play discusses the issues Azra's death raises.

2 (FAL) Refer to the notes on September 11 for ideas. Learners could use this as practice for summarising skills (LO2).

3 (HL) *She feels sick*: She is horrified at what has been done to a fellow Muslim woman. *Themes*: Gender bias; patriarchy.
She is defensive: People tend to feel sorry for women wearing scarves, assuming they have no choice. She too makes fun of them. *Themes*: Religious/racial stereotyping.

Wearing scarves: She wears a scarf, but not on her head, because of what it says – submission, male rule – and because she doesn't want to be labelled, or stereotyped. *Themes*: Gender bias; patriarchy.

4 Here is an example: Auntie Kariema blames the Jordanian girl's disobedience on the influence of Western music – a generalisation which Sara challenges by saying the girl couldn't have understood the English lyrics even if she did hear them. Auntie Kariema counters this by saying you can "*soema* just sense their sexy nonsense" and quickly goes on to another example, i.e. she says the singer Shakira must be a Muslim because of her name. This illustrates her way of making thoughtless generalisations.
Other prejudices or flawed reasoning to explore: leaving TV on because it's been paid for; Indian family's customs; Indian shopkeepers; that Azra is probably to blame for her actions, yet "I'm not saying she should have died".

5 The other girls look very Muslim/Arabic, with their straight hair and Eastern features, unlike Ayesha's more "African" looks. Although they look Muslim, she sees them as rather superficial. She doesn't look very Muslim, but has taken time to explore her spirituality. Their looks make them culturally acceptable, while hers might make others, like Auntie Kariema, discriminate against her.

6 Use the character summaries on pages 76–77 to check facts. Ask learners to read their responses aloud.

7 Ayesha talks about Muslim women in various countries, facing various forms of oppression, finally drawing us back to Cape Town. She has strong role models who "redefined the rules" here in Cape Town; yet says her "routes to freedom … have not yet been built". The implication is that this is even truer for those without strong role models, and with far less freedom. She leaves us with the question: "And where are my sisters?" – a question that has various possible interpretations, but whose answer must surely be "Everywhere".

Essay questions (pages 64–65)

These questions can be used for FAL and HL learners. FAL learners should write an essay of 150–200 words (Grade 10), 200–250 words (Grade 11), or 250–300 words (Grade 12) for 35 marks. HL learners should write an essay of 300–350 words (Grade 10), 350–400 words (Grade 11), or 400–450 words (Grade 12) for 25 marks. Consult the Subject Assessment Guidelines for further information.

1 Refer to the section on characters (pages 76–77), combined with the relevant synopsis for each monologue. Learners should give valid reasons, based on the character, for identifying with her. Note: boys can identify with a female character's values, characteristics, and so on.

2 The play consists of eleven monologues offered by six different women played by one actress. The play is unusual in that there is no real storyline with climax, and so on. The story begins and ends with Azra's death. In between these two scenes four different female characters develop the themes and what plot there is. Characters talk to invisible others, and the audience. Learners should comment on the relationships between characters, on the types of characters created, and on how they expand on the themes and plot, such as it is. The scenes between the opening and closing monologues are loosely strung along the month of Ramadan (learners should mention the link to themes) and are quite realistic in the way the women's lives intersect at various points.
Learners should expand on this basic structure to mention each character and how their monologues develop plot, theme, and characterisation.

3 The easiest way to trace the theme of gender bias, as it is expressed in the scarf, is to work through the play scene by scene.
Each scene begins with the actress wearing a scarf or using one in a different way – a powerful visual symbol, which should be discussed. Learners should say how the real scarf, together with the actress' movements, visually supports the aspect of gender bias dealt with in that particular scene. For example, in the opening scene Azra never removes the *hijab* (face covering) – this is a powerful visual symbol of how she is restricted by her community and religion.
Learners need to combine the material of the play into a coherent whole in order to focus on this topic. HL learners could regroup the material to deal with literal and then figurative elements.

4 Here is a list of the men and the themes they are linked to. Learners should not merely present a list, though; their answers should be in a well-structured essay.
stone-throwers (Azra's family and others) – human rights, gender discrimination; Fikkie, Auntie Kariema's husband – culture, tradition; Sara's Indian father – culture, tradition; Ayesha's one-time boyfriend, Nazeem – prejudice and racism; the phone customer who makes lewd suggestions to Tahira – culture, gender bias; Tahira's husband – culture, tradition; Mr Talbot – racism; boy at Eid and various men in Sara's poem – gender bias, culture, tradition; Auntie Kariema's father – tradition, gender bias (how easy was it for him to take his daughter home?); Madressa teacher – tradition.

Learners can comment on the fact that the final two scenes focus mainly on women. They need to combine the material of the play into a coherent whole in order to focus on this topic. FAL learners could keep the discussion chronological in terms of the play; HL learners should group the material in terms of themes or contrasting themes. This could be done in stages as learners rework the material and discuss it.

5 *The Scarf* (Monologue 2: Sara)
Structure: Quite a formal structure consisting of three statements, each followed by a verse. There is little rhyme, so what rhyme there is stands out, for example, noose/loose (see Monologue 2 answers for more discussion). Words to do with cloth and silk are used throughout the poem, echoing the title, "The Scarf".
Emotions and figurative language: Poetry allows words to be fitted together in unusual, less formal ways, such as "threads bright-woven/ heads misty-chained", where the word order is inverted. This is figurative language too – the scarves are not literally chains, but they represent an imprisoning attitude towards women.

Eid Day (Monologue 6: Sara)
Structure: There are three "scenes" that paint a clear picture of the activities, places, and people encountered on this day.
Emotions: Sara is speaking as a young man, giving us "his" perspective on this holiday.
Figurative language: "The mosque is full/of smiles and suits …"
There are fewer poetic devices, reflecting a more realistic scene. There is much colloquial language and slang, again reflecting the scenes described, particularly when the teenagers get together.

Ms Islam (Monologue 10: Ayesha)
Structure: Set to music, the poetry is much more structured in terms of a rhyme scheme, although this is not strict – the rhyme may be in lines 1 and 3, and 2 and 4, or only in lines 2 and 4, or only repetition of line endings. There is also repetition of words and phrases to emphasise certain points. At times a single word is placed on a line for effect, such as "locks" in dreadlocks (producing a second, figurative meaning to "locks"), and "Paradise".
Emotions: With Ayesha's slam poetry, music is used to reflect the emotions and support the rhythm of the poem. Hence the change in rhythm from being reflective at first, to becoming more demanding, questioning, urgent in tone and content.
Figurative language: "the voices woven into thread"; "maps made of silk".

General: The three fairly different styles of poetry, each serve their own purpose – to reflect and question, to describe a realistic scene, and to reflect and question again, this time more urgently and forcefully. All the elements of poetry are employed to various degrees, according to the poem's purpose.

Topics for discussion (pages 65–66)

1 "Ninja, 10 o'clock". A ninja is a person skilled in the traditional Japanese technique of espionage (spying) characterised by stealth and camouflage, often dressing in black; 10 o'clock is a reference to the position of a person in relation to an imagined analogue clock-face, usually used in war situations. Learners should discuss local stereotypes.

2 Learners should begin with identifying double standards in others, for example, parents, and should try to see double standards in their own lives too.
Sympathy for Tahira is fuelled by common ground such as being told how not to dress, having her cooking criticised, and so on.

3 Learners could mention various religious/cultural holidays and the emotions associated with them, and then link them to those of the play. They could also mention feelings about how we see/treat the elderly, and how they treat us.

4 *Terms to discuss*: African, coloured, white, European, black; race-names from other countries, such as nigger, African-American, and so on.

5 *Dress codes, food and holy places*: Learners could focus on the religions they have experienced or, after research, they could broaden the discussion. This links well with Life Orientation and Social Studies.
Possible holy places: Stonehenge (New Age/Druids); various Christian places of pilgrimage all over the world, from England (Canterbury) to France (Lourdes) to Israel (Jerusalem, Bethlehem) to South Africa (Moria – Zionist Church); Hindu sites in India (Ganges River); Tibetan monasteries; North American Indian sites; Australian Aboriginal sites (Uluru/Ayers Rock); African sites (Great Zimbabwe ruins/Mapungubwe).

6 The question gives guidelines for discussion – no further notes needed.

7 In war, the term "casualties" is often used, making the deaths less immediate, less "human". Reporting might also tend to use the passive voice, for example, "Twenty civilians were killed by aerial bombing in central Baghdad today." This removes or hides the doer of the action, in this case the soldier/country responsible for the killing. Terrorist attacks usually target civilians, specifically, rather than taking place in a war zone or battlefield where attacks are aimed at soldiers. Learners can give their own examples of such attacks.

8 Most religions, belief systems, and philosophies agree that people should treat others in a decent manner – treat others as you would like them to treat you.